Get Hooked on Crochet

Get Hooked on Crochet
FUN AND COLOURFUL PATTERNS FOR BEGINNERS

Natalie Beard

CICO BOOKS
LONDON NEW YORK

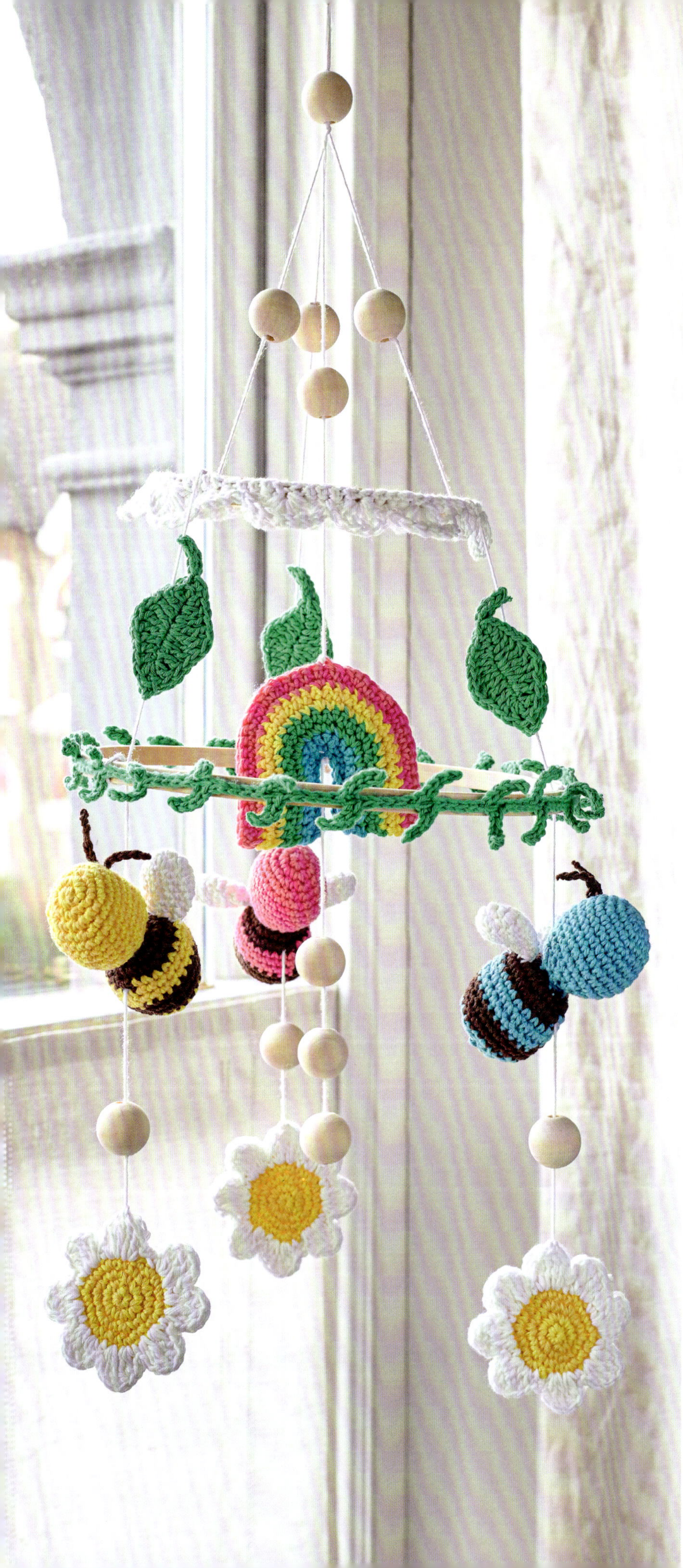

To my beautiful girls, Rosie, Martha, Violet and Audrey

Published in 2024 by CICO Books
an imprint of Ryland Peters & Small Ltd
20–21 Jockey's Fields, London WC1R 4BW

www.rylandpeters.com

10 9 8 7 6 5 4 3 2 1

Text © Natalie Beard 2024
Design, illustration, and photography
© CICO Books 2024

The designs in this book are copyright and must not be crocheted for sale.

The author's moral rights have been asserted. All rights reserved. No part of this publication may be reproduced, stored in a retrieval system or transmitted in any form or by any means, electronic, mechanical, photocopying or otherwise, without the prior permission of the publisher.

A CIP catalogue record for this book is available from the British Library.

ISBN: 978 1 80065 364 1

Printed in China

Editor: Marie Clayton
Pattern checker: Carol Ibbetson
Designer: Alison Fenton
Photographer: James Gardiner
Equipment photographer: Martin Norris
Stylist: Nel Haynes
Illustrator: Stephen Dew

In-house editor: Jenny Dye
Art director: Sally Powell
Creative director: Leslie Harrington
Production manager: Gordana Simakovic
Publishing manager: Carmel Edmonds

contents

Introduction 6
Tools and materials 8

CHAPTER 1
Colourful Homewares 10

Tea towel tidy 12
Flower cushion 14
Jam jar covers 17
Tulips stationery pot 20
Snail doorstop 22
Mushroom & acorn storage baskets 24
Rainbow rug 27
Granny stitch place mats and coasters 30
Caterpillar draught excluder 32
Granny square sofa tidy 34
Flower square wall tidy 37
Under the rainbow blanket 40
Table runner 44
Tissue box cover 46

CHAPTER 2
Cute Accessories & Gifts 48

Bookmarks 50
Peg dolls 53
Lavender heart 56
Mug cosy 58
Fridge magnets 60
Ladybird and flower coasters 63
Little house hot water bottle cover 66
Pencil toppers 69
Gnome sweet gnome bookends 72
Mushroom home keyring 76
Strawberry water bottle cover 78
Sunshine and snails game 81

CHAPTER 3
Beautiful Wreaths & Decorations 84

Bee and flower mobile 86
Mushroom wall décor 90
Blooming lovely flower pot 94
Daisy chain mirror 98
Roses garland 100
Daisy chain bunting 102
Frilly crochet chain 104
Rainbow wreath 106
Gnome's washing wreath 110

Techniques 114
Abbreviations 126
Suppliers & Acknowledgements 127
Index 128

introduction

I'm Natalie, a mum of four beautiful girls, and I am absolutely hooked on creating quirky crochet designs to entertain and make people smile.

I've loved to craft since I was little, and I have my mum to thank for that. I have early, happy memories of her pottery and her charcoal and pen-and-ink drawings filling our home. She still loves to knit for me and my daughters, and there's nothing quite like a cherished homemade gift.

Sadly, I lost my dad two months before having my third daughter, and I picked up a crochet hook as a means of coping with the mixed emotions from losing my dad and gaining a gorgeous new baby. I truly believe crochet is a happy distraction from day-to-day stresses, and is so good for our mental health and wellbeing, allowing you to escape to a squish-filled happy place!

I had my first commission from Hobbycraft, and then had the pleasure of designing for Knitcraft (Hobbycraft's sister company). After being made redundant from my day job of 13 years, I decided to turn the negative into a positive and focus on crochet full-time! Ever since, I have been honoured to work with lots of different yarn companies, and have been on the design team for *Simply Crochet* magazine. I now also work as a Hobbycraft Artisan in store, where I host workshops.

My passion for crochet and all things yarny has grown into a total squishy obsession and I rarely go a day without getting my hook out. I hope you'll enjoy my yarn-filled adventure through the pages of my first-ever book, feel inspired to pick up your hook and have heaps of fun making!

BEFORE YOU BEGIN

If you are new to crochet, check out the Techniques section on pages 114–125 and the Abbreviations on page 126. On page 8, you'll find a guide to the tools you'll need. Each of the projects has a skill rating, from Very Easy (one circle) to Easy (two circles) and Intermediate (three circles). Start with the Very Easy patterns, then move on to the next two levels once you know the basic techniques.

tools and materials

Here is a guide to the basic tools and materials you will need to make the projects in this book.

CROCHET HOOKS

A crochet hook is a simple tool that is shaped to fit in the hand and glide easily in and out of the crochet loops. Modern crochet hooks are made in bamboo, wood, aluminium, steel, casein or plastic. Some have handles made of plastic and many have a flat piece around the centre of the length of the hook, which is a thumb guide.

The choice of hook is up to you, but the varnish on bamboo crochet hooks can wear off after a while and they then catch on the yarn. You may find that an ergonomic hook with a round plastic handle (shown above) is more comfortable. Whichever type of hook you choose, it's important that it has a good smooth tip – for this reason alone it's worth buying one of the more expensive brands.

Crochet hooks come in a variety of sizes and you'll be guided by the pattern and the thickness of yarn as to which size you need.

OTHER TOOLS

As well your crochet hook, there are a few extra tools that you will need.

SHARP SCISSORS

Reserved for cutting yarn and thread only: do not cut paper with these, because it will quickly blunt them.

TAPE MEASURE
You will need this to block some of the finished projects to the finished size (see page 120).

PINS
Use rustproof, glass-headed or T-headed quilters' pins for blocking and to pin crocheted pieces together before you join them (see pages 120–122). Bright-coloured tops will prevent the pins getting lost in the crocheted fabric.

YARN

Yarns come in different thicknesses or weights. The five basic types, from lightest to heaviest, are 4-ply (fingering), double-knitting or DK (light worsted), Aran (worsted), chunky (bulky), and super-chunky (super-bulky). The finer the yarn, the smaller the hook size that is needed – the pattern will suggest a suitable hook size. Most ball bands will also suggest a suitable hook size for the yarn.

Yarns are available in a variety of different fibres, from acrylic to natural fibres such as 100% wool, alpaca, cashmere, cotton, mohair and bamboo, as well as mixes of different fibres. Acrylic is synthetic and manufactured to imitate wool yarn. Its advantages are that it is cheaper than wool and other natural fibres, and can be put in the washing machine. Cotton is a soft and strong yarn, and it makes a very sturdy and consistent crocheted fabric. Natural yarns such as wool, cashmere, alpaca and mohair are softer and warmer. They are more delicate and will often need to be hand-washed.

If you wish, you can use different yarns to the ones recommended in this book, but you will need a yarn with the same recommended hook size as the pattern (see the Yarnsub website on page 127 to help you). Many of the patterns in this book use only a small amount of each colour, so they're ideal for using up yarn from your stash.

STITCH MARKERS
These aren't essential but are useful for clipping onto your working loop when you're taking a break partway through a project so that it doesn't unravel. They're also handy for keeping track of how many chains you've made when starting a project and for marking the start of a round.

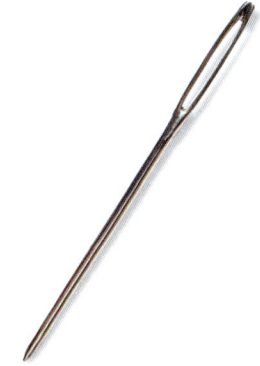

YARN NEEDLE
This type of needle is longer and thicker than a sewing needle. The blunt end will not split the yarn when sewing up and the large eye makes it easier to thread with yarn.

tools and materials

CHAPTER 1
Colourful Homewares

Brighten up your kitchen with this eye-catching and useful tea towel holder. Featuring floral granny squares, this design can be worked in any colourway and is perfect for using up leftover yarn from other projects.

tea towel tidy

SKILL RATING ● ● ○

YARN AND MATERIALS
Rico Ricorumi DK (100% cotton) DK (light worsted) weight yarn, 58m (64yd) per 25g (1oz) ball
  1 ball in each of:
    Yellow 006 (A)
    Sky Blue 031 (B)
    Red 028 (C)
    Green 049 (D)
2 natural wooden rings, 5cm (2in) diameter

HOOK AND EQUIPMENT
3mm (US size C/2-D/3) crochet hook
Yarn needle

FINISHED MEASUREMENT
19cm (7½in) long when folded incl rings x 9cm (3½in) wide

ABBREVIATIONS
See page 126.

HANGER
SQUARE
(make 2 in diff colours as specified) Using A or B, make a magic ring.
Round 1: Ch3 (counts as 1tr), 11tr in magic ring. *(12 tr)*
Fasten off A, join C. Fasten off B, join A.
Round 2: Ch2 (does not count as a st), tr5tog in first st, ch2, [tr5tog in next st, ch2] 11 times, slst to first tr in beg tr5tog. *(12-tr cluster, 5 x ch-2)*
Fasten off C, join B. Fasten off A, join C.
Round 3: (Ch3 (counts as 1tr), 2tr, ch3, 3tr) in ch sp, [3htr in next ch sp] twice, *(3tr, ch3, 3tr) in next ch sp, [3htr in next ch sp] twice, rep from * twice more, slst in third ch of beg ch-3. Fasten off all colours, join D to corner ch sp.
Round 4: (Ch3 (counts as first tr), 2tr, ch3, 3tr) in corner ch sp, [3tr in next ch sp] 3 times, *(3tr, ch3, 3tr) in corner ch sp, [3tr in next ch sp] 3 times, rep from * twice more, slst in third ch of beg ch. Fasten off. Sew in ends (see page 120), sew two squares tog along one edge, using mattress stitch (see page 121).

ENDS
(make 2, working on opp short sides of rectangle)
With RS facing, join D to first st.
Row 1: Ch1, 1dc in each st to end, 1dc in ch sp, ch1, turn. *(16 dc)*
Row 2: 1dc in each st to end, ch1, turn.
Row 3: Dc2tog, 12dc, dc2tog, ch1, turn. *(14 dc)*
Row 4: 1dc in each st to end, ch1, turn.
Row 5: Dc2tog, 10dc, dc2tog, ch1, turn. *(12 dc)*
Row 6: 1dc in each st to end, ch1, turn.
Row 7: Dc2tog, 8dc, dc2tog, ch1, turn. *(10 dc)*
Row 8: 1dc in each st to end, ch1, turn.
Round 9: Dc2tog, 6dc, dc2tog, ch1, turn. *(8 dc)*
Round 10: 1dc in each st to end, ch1, turn.
Round 11: Dc2tog, 4dc, dc2tog, ch1, turn. *(6 dc)*
Round 12: 1dc in each st to end, ch1, turn.
Rounds 13-17: 1dc in each st to end, ch1, turn.
Round 18: 1dc in each st to end. Fasten off, leaving long tail to sew around a wooden ring.
Rep on opp side.
Border: 1dc in each st and row end around all sides.
Fasten off.

FINISHING
Fold end over wooden ring and sew in place. Rep with second ring on other end of hanger.

flower cushion

Add a burst of colour to any room with this unique cushion. The circular pattern features a repeated 3D-petal effect, making this cushion a statement piece for your home. Choose a selection of chunky yarns in bold contrasting shades.

SKILL RATING ● ● ○

YARN AND MATERIALS
Women's Institute Soft and Chunky (70% acrylic, 30% merino wool) chunky (bulky) weight yarn, 110m (120yd) per 100g (3½oz) ball
- 1 ball in each of:
  - Mustard (A)
  - Dusky Pink (B)
  - Pink (C)
- 2 balls of Petrol (D)

45cm (17½in) diameter circular cushion pad

HOOK AND EQUIPMENT
8mm (US size L/11) crochet hook
Yarn needle

FINISHED MEASUREMENTS
45cm (17½in) diameter
NOTE: First 3 rounds of front and back panels should measure approx. 15cm (6in).

ABBREVIATIONS
See page 126.

SPECIAL ABBREVIATION
Puff st (puff stitch): Yrh insert hook into specified st/sp, yrh and pull up a long loop, [yrh, insert hook in same st/sp, yrh and pull up a long loop] 3 times, yrh and pull through all 9 loops on hook, ch1 to close Puff st.

CUSHION
FLOWER
Using A, make a magic ring.
Round 1: Ch3 (counts as first tr), 11tr in magic ring, slst in third ch of beg ch. *(12 tr)*
Round 2: Working between tr from prev round, ch2 (does not count as st), [puff st, ch2] 12 times, slst in top of first puff st. *(12 puff sts, 12 x ch-2)*
Round 3: Ch2 (does not count as a st), [2htr in ch-2 sp, 1htr in puff st] 12 times, slst in first htr. *(36 htr)*
Fasten off A, join B.
Round 4: Ch1, [BPslst around htr, ch3, miss next htr] 18 times, slst to first slst.
Round 5: Working in each ch-3 sp from prev round, [slst into next ch-3 sp, ch3, 2tr, ch3, slst in same ch-3 sp] 18 times. Fasten off.
Round 6: Using B, join and work in missed htrs from Round 4, ch 1, [BPslst around htr, ch4, miss next htr] 18 times, slst to first slst.
Round 7: Working in each ch-4 sp from prev round, [slst into next ch-4 sp, ch4, 3dtr, ch4, slst in same 4-ch sp] 18 times. Fasten off B, join C around a slst from prev round.
Round 8: Working in BPslst from Round 7, [BPslst, ch3] 18 times, slst into first slst.
Round 9: Slst into next ch-3 sp, ch2 (does not count as a st), 3htr in same ch-3 sp, [3htr in next ch-3 sp] 17 times, slst into first htr. *(54 htr)*

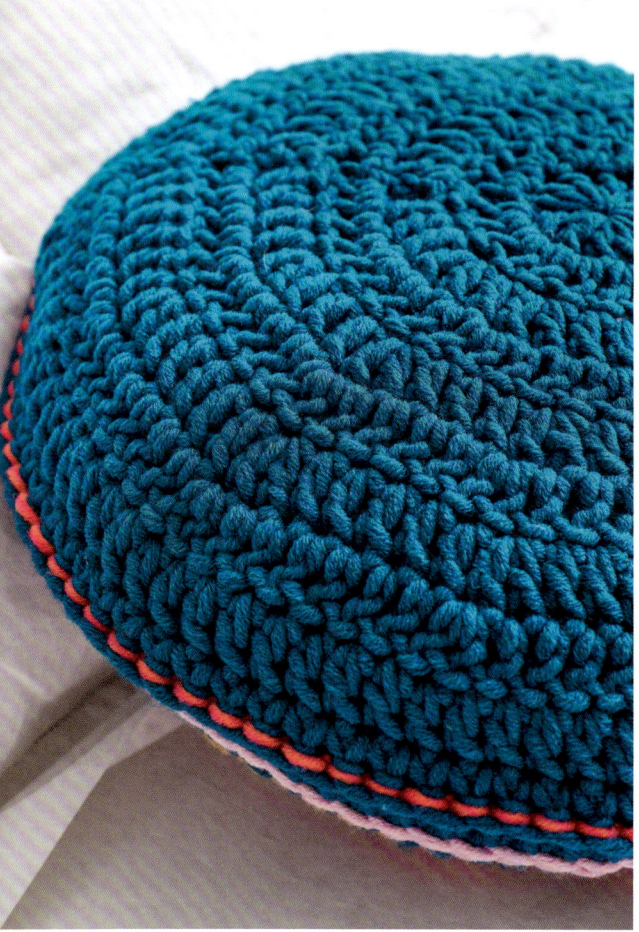

Round 10: (Ch4, miss 2 htr, slst in next htr), 18 times, slst into first st.
Round 11: Working in each ch-4 sp from prev round, [slst into next ch-4 sp, ch3, 2tr, ch3, slst in same ch-4 sp] 18 times.
Round 12: Working in slst from Round 11 [BPslst, ch6, miss next slst] 9 times, slst in first BPslst.
Round 13: Working in ch-6 sp from prev round, [slst into next ch-6 sp, ch4, 5dtr, ch4, slst in same ch-6 sp] 9 times.
Fasten off and sew in ends.

FRONT AND BACK PANELS
(make 2)
Using D, make a magic ring.
Round 1: Ch3 (counts as 1tr throughout), 11tr in magic ring, slst in third ch of beg ch. *(12 tr)*
Round 2: Ch3, 1tr in same st, [2tr in next st] 11 times, slst in third ch of beg ch. *(24 tr)*
Round 3: Ch3, 2tr in next st, [1tr, 2tr in next st] 11 times, slst in third ch of beg ch. *(36 tr)*
Round 4: Ch3, 1tr, 2tr in next st, [2tr, 2tr in next st] 11 times, slst in third ch of beg ch. *(48 tr)*
Round 5: Ch3, 2tr, 2tr in next st, [3tr, 2tr in next st] 11 times, slst in third ch of beg ch. *(60 tr)*
Round 6: Ch3, 3tr, 2tr in next st, [4tr, 2tr in next st] 11 times, slst in third ch of beg ch. *(72 tr)*
Round 7: Ch3, 4tr, 2tr in next st, [5tr, 2tr in next st] 11 times, slst in third ch of beg ch. *(84 tr)*
Round 8: Ch3, 5tr, 2tr in next st, [6tr, 2tr in next st] 11 times, slst in third ch of beg ch. *(96 tr)*
Round 9: Ch3, 95tr, slst in third ch of beg ch. *(96 tr)*
Fasten off and sew in ends (see page 12).

FINISHING
Work line of surface crochet (see page 123) using A in top of each st in Round 7 and B in top of each st in Round 8 of front panel. Sew flower motif on front panel.
With front and back panels WS tog, using D work dc through each st around, placing cushion pad inside before completing seam (see page 122).
Work line of surface crochet using C in joining round.
Fasten off and sew in ends.

Featuring cute strawberry and flower motifs, these jar covers would add a pop of colour to your kitchen shelf. They also make wonderful gifts on top of jars of honey or homemade jam.

jam jar covers

SKILL RATING ● ● ○

YARN AND MATERIALS
Rico Ricorumi DK (100% cotton)
DK (light worsted) weight yarn,
58m (64yd) per 25g (1oz) ball
1 ball in each of:
  Sky Blue 031 (A)
  Fuchsia 014 (B)
  Yellow 006 (C)
  Green 049 (D)
  Red 028 (E)
  White 001 (F)

HOOK AND EQUIPMENT
3mm (US size C/2-D/3) crochet hook
Yarn needle

FINISHED MEASUREMENT
14cm (5½in) diameter

ABBREVIATIONS
See page 126.

COVER
(make 1 in A, 1 in B)
Make a magic ring.
Round 1: 6dc in magic ring. *(6 dc)*
Round 2: [2dc in next st] 6 times. *(12 dc)*
Round 3: [1dc, 2dc in next st] 6 times. *(18 dc)*
Round 4: [2dc, 2dc in next st] 6 times. *(24 dc)*
Round 5: [3dc, 2dc in next st] 6 times. *(30 dc)*
Round 6: [4dc, 2dc in next st] 6 times. *(36 dc)*
Round 7: [5dc, 2dc in next st] 6 times. *(42 dc)*
Round 8: [6dc, 2dc in next st] 6 times. *(48 dc)*
Round 9: [7dc, 2dc in next st] 6 times. *(54 dc)*
Round 10: [8dc, 2dc in next st] 6 times. *(60 dc)*
Round 11: [9dc, 2dc in next st] 6 times. *(66 dc)*
Round 12: [1dc, ch2, miss 1 st] to end, slst in first dc.
Fasten off and sew in ends.

CORD
(make 1 in C, 1 in D)
Ch80.
Fasten off.

STRAWBERRY
Using E, make a magic ring.
Round 1: Ch3 (counts as 1tr), 12tr, slst in third ch of beg ch. *(13 tr)*
Round 2: Miss first st, (1htr, 1tr) in next tr, [3dtr in next tr] twice, [3tr in next tr] twice, (2tr, 1dtr) in next tr, ch1, (1dtr, 2tr) in next tr, [3tr in next tr] twice, [3dtr in next tr] twice, (1tr, 1htr) in next tr, slst in first st.
Fasten off leaving long tail to sew to cover.

STALK
Using D.
Round 1: [Ch4, 1dc in second ch from hook, 1dc in each of next 2 ch] 3 times, slst in first st.
Fasten off leaving long tail to sew to strawberry.

18 colourful homewares

FLOWER
Using C, make a magic ring.
Round 1: 6dc in magic ring. *(6 dc)*
Round 2: [2dc in next st] 6 times. *(12 dc)*
Round 3: [1dc, 2dc in next st] 6 times. *(18 dc)*
Fasten off C, join F.
Round 4: *(1dc, ch3, 2dtr) in next dc, (2dtr, ch3, 1dc) in next dc, 1dc in next dc; rep from * 5 more times, slst to first dc.
Fasten off leaving long tail to sew to cover.

FINISHING
Weave cord through Round 10 of each cover, leaving 3 dc between in and out points. Tie ends in bow.
With a small amount of F, stitch simple seeds onto strawberry before sewing onto first cover. Sew stalk to base of strawberry. Sew flower onto top of second cover.

tulips stationery pot

Transform a simple tin can into a pretty stationery pot for your desk. As well as simple stripes crocheted in basic double crochet, this design uses three-treble clusters to create the raised tulip flower pattern.

SKILL RATING ● ● ○

YARN AND MATERIALS
Knitcraft Cotton Blend DK (50% cotton, 50% acrylic) DK (light worsted) weight yarn, 215m (235yd) per 100g (3½oz) ball
   1 ball in each of:
   Yellow 1008 (A)
   Teal 1002 (B)
   Hot Pink 1003 (C)

Tin can

HOOK AND EQUIPMENT
4mm (US size G/6) crochet hook

Yarn needle

FINISHED MEASUREMENTS
11cm (4¼in) tall by 25.5cm (10in) circumference

ABBREVIATIONS
See page 126.

SPECIAL ABBREVIATION
3trCL (three-treble cluster): yrh, insert hook in st, yrh, pull through (3 loops on hook), yrh, pull through first 2 loops on hook (2 loops on hook), yrh, insert hook in same st, yrh, pull through (4 loops on hook), yrh, pull through first 2 loops on hook (3 loops on hook), yrh, insert hook in same st, yrh, pull through (5 loops on hook), yrh, pull through first 2 loops on hook (4 loops on hook), yrh, pull through all 4 loops on hook.

COVER
Worked from base up.

Using A, make a magic ring.

Round 1: 6dc in magic ring. *(6 sts)*
Round 2: [2dc in next st] 6 times. *(12 sts)*
Round 3: [1dc, 2dc in next st] 6 times. *(18 sts)*
Round 4: [2dc, 2dc in next st] 6 times. *(24 sts)*
Round 5: [3dc, 2dc in next st] 6 times. *(30 sts)*
Round 6: [4dc, 2dc in next st] 6 times. *(36 sts)*
Round 7: 1dcBLO in each st around.
Rounds 8–10: 1dc in each st around.
Fasten off A, join B.
Round 11: Ch4 (counts as 1tr, ch1), 1tr in same st, miss 2 dc, *(1tr, ch1, 1tr) in next st, miss 2 dc; rep from * 10 more times, slst in third ch of beg 4-ch.
Fasten off B, join C in a ch sp.
Round 12: Ch2 (does not count as st), [3trCL in ch sp, ch3] 12 times. *(12 tulips)*
Fasten off C, join A.
Round 13: 3dc in each ch sp around. *(36 sts)*
Round 14: 1dc in each st around.
Fasten off A, join B.
Rounds 15 and 16: 1dc in each st around.
Fasten off B, join A.
Rounds 17 and 18: 1dc in each st around.
Fasten off A, join B.
Round 19: Rep Round 11.
Fasten off B, join C.
Round 20: Rep Round 12.
Fasten off C, join A.
Round 21: Rep Round 13.
Rounds 22 and 23: 1dc in each st around.
Fasten off and sew in ends (see page 120).

FINISHING
Place cover over tin.

snail doorstop

This cute character would add a playful touch to your home or a child's bedroom. The different colours in the yarn add gorgeous details to the crocheted fabric, but you could use any chunky yarn. Why not try using different shades from your stash on the snail's spiral shell for a multicoloured effect?

SKILL RATING ● ○ ○

YARN AND MATERIALS
Knitcraft Join the Dots Chunky (80% acrylic, 20% wool) chunky (bulky) weight yarn, 190m (208yd) per 100g (3½oz) ball
  1 ball in each of:
   Purple Print 1000 (A)
   Cream Print 1002 (B)
Fibre filling
Weighted filling for base of body
Pair of 8mm (½in) black safety eyes

HOOK AND EQUIPMENT
5mm (US size H/8) crochet hook
Yarn needle

FINISHED MEASUREMENTS
30cm (11¾in) wide maximum, by 18cm (7in) tall

ABBREVIATIONS
See page 126.

SNAIL
SHELL
Using A, make a magic ring.
Round 1: 6dc in magic ring. *(6 sts)*
Round 2: [2dc in next st] 6 times. *(12 sts)*
Round 3: [1dc, 2dc in next st] 6 times. *(18 sts)*
Round 4: [2dc, 2dc in next st] 6 times. *(24 sts)*
Round 5: [3dc, 2dc in next st] 6 times. *(30 sts)*
Round 6: [4dc, 2dc in next st] 6 times. *(36 sts)*
Round 7: [5dc, 2dc in next st] 6 times. *(42 sts)*
Round 8: [6dc, 2dc in next st] 6 times. *(48 sts)*
Round 9: [7dc, 2dc in next st] 6 times. *(54 sts)*
Round 10: [8dc, 2dc in next st] 6 times. *(60 sts)*
Round 11: 1dcBLO in each st around.
Rounds 12 and 13: 1dc in each st around.
Fasten off and sew in ends (see page 120).
Repeat Rounds 1–10 for other side of shell.
Fasten off leaving a long tail to sew to first part of shell.

BODY
Using B, make a magic ring.
Round 1: 6dc in magic ring. *(6 sts)*
Round 2: [2dc in next st] 6 times. *(12 sts)*
Round 3: [1dc, 2dc in next st] 6 times. *(18 sts)*
Start to stuff with fibre filling until Round 22, do not stuff between Rounds 22–42, then stuff between Rounds 43–48.
Rounds 4–44: 1dc in each st around.
Insert safety eyes between Rounds 6 and 7, 4 sts apart.
Round 45: [1dc, dc2tog] 6 times. *(12 sts)*
Rounds 46 and 47: 1dc in each st around.
Round 48: [Dc2tog] 6 times. *(6 sts)*
Fasten off and sew closed.

22 colourful homewares

ANTENNAE
Using B, ch15.
Row 1: Slst in second ch from hook, 13slst. *(14 slst)*
Sew in ends.

FINISHING
Sew both parts of shell together, stitching in back loops only. Fill with fibre filling and weighted filling before sewing closed. Sew in ends.
Thread antennae strip through top of head, between Rounds 1 and 2, and sew in place. Sew shell to body.

snail doorstop

mushroom & acorn storage baskets

Perfect for storing anything from toys and stationery to yarn and craft supplies, these baskets would make fun additions to any room. Worked in chunky cotton yarn, they are quick and simple to make. The crab stitch detailing around each lid creates a twisted, rounded edge.

SKILL RATING ● ● ○

YARN AND MATERIALS
Knitcraft Return Of Mac Yarn (100% cotton) chunky (bulky) weight yarn, 81m (88½yd) per 200g (7oz) ball

For Mushroom Storage Basket:
　1 ball in Terracotta (A)
　2 balls in Ecru (B)
　Small amount of Khaki (C)

For Acorn Storage Basket:
　1 ball in Khaki (C)
　2 balls in Linen (D)
　Small amount of Terracotta (A)

2 pairs of 22mm black safety eyes

HOOK AND EQUIPMENT
10mm (US size N/15) crochet hook
Yarn needle

FINISHED MEASUREMENTS
Mushroom basket: 15cm (6in) diameter x 25cm (9¾in) tall

Acorn basket: 15cm (6in) diameter x 18cm (7in) tall

ABBREVIATIONS
See page 126.

SPECIAL ABBREVIATION
Waistcoat st (waistcoat stitch): Work each dc in V between sts.
Crab st (crab stitch): Ch1, insert hook in st to right, yrh and pull through (2 loops on hook) yrh, pull through 2 loops.

MUSHROOM STORAGE BASKET
CAP
Work in waistcoat st throughout.
Using A, make a magic ring.
Round 1: 6dc in magic ring. *(6 dc)*
Round 2: [2dc in next st] 6 times. *(12 dc)*
Round 3: 1dc in each st around.
Round 4: [1dc, 2dc in next st] 6 times. *(18 dc)*
Round 5: 1dc in each st around.
Round 6: [2dc, 2dc in next st] 6 times. *(24 dc)*
Round 7: 1dc in each st around.
Round 8: [3dc, 2dc in next st] 6 times. *(30 dc)*
Round 9: 1dc in each st around.
Round 10: [4dc, 2dc in next st] 6 times. *(36 dc)*
Round 11: 1dc in each st around.
Round 12: [5dc, 2dc in next st] 6 times. *(42 dc)*
Round 13: 1dc in each st around.
Round 14: [6dc, 2dc in next st] 6 times. *(48 dc)*
Round 15: 1dc in each st around.
Round 16: [7dc, 2dc in next st] 6 times. *(60 dc)*
Round 17: 1dc in each st around.
Round 18: Crab st in each st to end. *(60 sts)*
Fasten off and sew in ends (see page 120).

BASE
Work in waistcoat st throughout.
Using B, make a magic ring.
Round 1: 6dc in magic ring. *(6 dc)*
Round 2: [2dc in next st] 6 times. *(12 dc)*
Round 3: [1dc, 2dc in next st] 6 times. *(18 dc)*
Round 4: [2dc, 2dc in next st] 6 times. *(24 dc)*
Round 5: [3dc, 2dc in next st] 6 times. *(30 dc)*
Round 6: [4dc, 2dc in next st] 6 times. *(36 dc)*
Round 7: [5dc, 2dc in next st] 6 times. *(42 dc)*

Round 8: 1dcBLO in each st around.
Rounds 9-21: 1dc in each st around.
Round 22: Crab st in each st to end. *(42 sts)*
Fasten off and sew in ends.

SMALL SPOTS
(make 3)
Using B, make a magic ring.
Round 1: 6dc in magic ring. *(6 dc)*
Fasten off leaving long tail to sew to cap.

LARGE SPOTS
(make 2)
Using B, make a magic ring.
Round 1: 6dc in magic ring. *(6 dc)*
Round 2: [2dc in next st] 6 times. *(12 dc)*
Fasten off leaving long tail to sew to cap.

FINISHING
Insert safety eyes between Rounds 13 and 14 of base, 6 sts apart.
Using a small amount of C, sew a simple mouth between Rounds 13 and 14 of base, across 3 sts.
Sew spots onto cap.

ACORN STORAGE BASKET
ACORN CAP
Work in waistcoat st throughout.
Using C, make a magic ring.
Round 1: 6dc in magic ring. *(6 dc)*
Round 2: [2dc in next st] 6 times. *(12 dc)*
Round 3: [1dc, 2dc in next st] 6 times. *(18 dc)*
Round 4: [2dc, 2dc in next st] 6 times. *(24 dc)*
Round 5: [3dc, 2dc in next st] 6 times. *(30 dc)*
Round 6: [4dc, 2dc in next st] 6 times. *(36 dc)*
Round 7: [5dc, 2dc in next st] 6 times. *(42 dc)*
Round 8: [6dc, 2dc in next st] 6 times. *(48 dc)*
Rounds 9-15: 1dc in each st around.
Round 16: Crab st in each st to end. *(48 sts)*
Fasten off and sew in ends.

ACORN STALK
Using C, ch4.
Row 1: Slst in second ch from hook, 2slst. *(3 sts)*
Fasten off leaving a long tail to sew to cap.

ACORN
Work in waistcoat st throughout.
Using D, make a magic ring.
Round 1: 6dc in magic ring. *(6 dc)*
Round 2: [2dc in next st] 6 times. *(12 dc)*
Round 3: 1dc in each st around.
Round 4: [1dc, 2dc in next st] 6 times. *(18 dc)*
Round 5: [2dc, 2dc in next st] 6 times. *(24 dc)*
Round 6: [3dc, 2dc in next st] 6 times. *(30 dc)*
Round 7: [4dc, 2dc in next st] 6 times. *(36 dc)*
Round 8: [5dc, 2dc in next st] 6 times. *(42 dc)*
Rounds 9-25: 1dc in each st around.
Round 26: Crab st in each st to end. *(42 sts)*
Fasten off and sew in ends.

FINISHING
Insert safety eyes between Rounds 12 and 13 of acorn, 6 sts apart.
Using a small amount of A, sew a simple mouth between Rounds 12 and 13 of acorn, across 3 sts.
Sew acorn stalk to top of acorn cap.

Add a gorgeous handmade detail to a bedroom or nursery with this multicoloured rug. Crocheted with three strands of DK yarn held together, the pattern works up quickly and is finished with a pretty white edging. Choose bright shades like this version, or experiment with colour by using pastel rainbow yarns.

rainbow rug

SKILL RATING ● ○ ○

YARN AND MATERIALS
Women's Institute Premium Acrylic Yarn (100% acrylic) DK (light worsted) weight yarn, 250m (273yd) per 100g (3½oz) ball
  1 ball in each of:
  Bright Lilac 1007 (A)
  Soft Blue 1025 (B)
  Green 1001 (C)
  Yellow 1025 (D)
  Orange 1002 (E)
  Red 1015 (F)
  Soft Pink 1026 (G)
  White 1000 (H)

HOOK AND EQUIPMENT
8mm (US size L/11) crochet hook
Yarn needle

FINISHED MEASUREMENTS
Straight edge: 85cm (33½in)
Radius: 46cm (18in)

ABBREVIATIONS
See page 126.

RUG
Use three strands of each colour held together.
Using A, ch7.
Row 1 (RS): 1dc in second ch from hook, 4dc, 3dc in last ch, working along opp side of chain, 5dc, turn. (*13 dc*)
Row 2: Ch1 (does not count as st throughout), 5dc, [2dc in next st] 3 times, 5dc, turn. (*16 dc*)
Row 3: Ch1, 5dc, [1dc, 2dc in next st] 3 times, 5dc, turn. (*19 dc*)
Row 4: Ch1, 5dc, [2dc, 2dc in next st] 3 times, 5dc, turn. (*22 dc*)
Row 5: Ch1, 5dc, [3dc, 2dc in next st] 3 times, 5dc, turn. (*25 dc*)
Fasten off A, join B.
Row 6: Ch1, 5dc, [4dc, 2dc in next st] 3 times, 5dc, turn. (*28 dc*)
Row 7: Ch1, 5dc, [5dc, 2dc in next st] 3 times, 5dc, turn. (*31 dc*)
Row 8: Ch1, 8dc, 2dc in next st, [6dc, 2dc in next st] twice, 8dc, turn. (*34 dc*)
Row 9: Ch1, 5dc, [7dc, 2dc in next st] 3 times, 5dc, turn. (*37 dc*)
Row 10: Ch1, 9dc, 2dc in next st, [8dc, 2dc in next st] twice, 9dc, turn. (*40 dc*)
Fasten off B, join C.
Row 11: Ch1, 5dc, [9dc, 2dc in next st] 3 times, 5dc, turn. (*43 dc*)
Row 12: Ch1, [10dc, 2dc in next st] 3 times, 10dc, turn. (*46 dc*)
Row 13: Ch1, 5dc, [11dc, 2dc in next st] 3 times, 5dc, turn. (*49 dc*)
Row 14: Ch1, 11dc, 2dc in next st, [12dc, 2dc in next st] twice, 11dc, turn. (*52 dc*)
Row 15: Ch1, 5dc, [13dc, 2dc in next st] 3 times, 5dc, turn. (*55 dc*)
Fasten off C, join D.
Row 16: Ch1, 13dc, 2dc in next st, [14dc, 2dc in next st] twice, 11dc, turn. (*58 dc*)
Row 17: Ch1, 5dc, [15dc, 2dc in next st] 3 times, 5dc, turn. (*61 dc*)

Row 18: Ch1, 13dc, 2dc in next st, [16dc, 2dc in next st] twice, 13dc, turn. (*64 dc*)
Row 19: Ch1, 5dc, [17dc, 2dc in next st] 3 times, 5dc, turn. (*67 dc*)
Row 20: Ch1, 14dc, 2dc in next st, [18dc, 2dc in next st] twice, 14dc, turn. (*70 dc*)
Fasten off D, join E.
Row 21: Ch1, 5dc, [19dc, 2dc in next st] 3 times, 5dc, turn. (*73 dc*)
Row 22: Ch1, 15dc, 2dc in next st, [20dc, 2dc in next st] twice, 15dc, turn. (*76 dc*)
Row 23: Ch1, 5dc, [21dc, 2dc in next st] 3 times, 5dc, turn. (*79 dc*)
Row 24: Ch1, 16dc, 2dc in next st, [22dc, 2dc in next st] twice, 10dc, 2dc in next st, 5dc, turn. (*83 dc*)
Row 25: Ch1, 5dc, [23dc, 2dc in next st] 3 times, 6dc, turn. (*86 dc*)
Fasten off E, join F.
Row 26: Ch1, 17dc, 2dc in next st, [24dc, 2dc in next st] twice, 12dc, 2dc in next st, 5dc, turn. (*90 dc*)
Row 27: Ch1, 5dc, [25dc, 2dc in next st] 3 times, 7dc, turn. (*93 dc*)
Row 28: Ch1, 18dc, 2dc in next st, [26dc, 2dc in next st] twice, 13dc, 2dc in next st, 6dc, turn. (*97 dc*)
Row 29: Ch1, 5dc, [27dc, 2dc in next st] twice, 30dc, 2dc in next st, 5dc, turn. (*100 dc*)
Row 30: Ch1, 19dc, 2dc in next st, [28dc, 2dc in next st] twice, 14dc, 2dc in next st, 7dc, turn. (*104 dc*)
Fasten off F, join G.

Row 31: Ch1, 74dc, 2dc in next st, 23dc, 2dc in next st, 5dc, turn. (*106 dc*)
Row 32: Ch1, 20dc, 2dc in next st, [30dc, 2dc in next st] twice, 17dc, 2dc in next st, 5dc, turn. (*110 dc*)
Row 33: Ch1, 41dc, 2dc in next st, 36dc, 2dc in next st, 25dc, 2dc in next st, 5dc, turn. (*113 dc*)
Row 34: Ch1, 21dc, 2dc in next st, [32dc, 2dc in next st] twice, 19dc, 2dc in next st, 5dc, turn. (*117 dc*)
Row 35: Ch1, 38dc, 2dc in next st, 37dc, 2dc in next st, 34dc, 2dc in next st, 5dc, turn. (*120 dc*)
Fasten off G.
With RS facing, join H to the bottom right corner.
Round 36: Ch1, (1dc, ch3, 1dc) in first corner, [ch3, miss 1 st, 1dc] 59 times, (1dc, ch3, 1dc) in next corner, [ch3, miss 1 row end, 1dc in next row end] 34 times, ch3, miss 1 row end, sl st in first st to join.
Fasten off.

FINISHING
Sew in all ends (see page 120).

granny stitch place mats and coasters

Try out the classic granny stitch with this simple and bold pattern. Mix and match your colours for each mat, or create co-ordinating ones with just two shades. A set of these place mats and coasters would make a lovely housewarming gift.

PLACE MAT

Using main colour, make a magic ring.
Round 1: Ch3 (counts as first tr throughout), 2tr in ring, ch1, [3tr in ring, ch1] 5 times, slst in third ch of beg ch to join. (*six 3tr groups*)
Work in ch sp between tr groups from prev rounds throughout.
Round 2: Ch3 in first ch sp, [(3tr, ch1, 3tr) in next ch sp, ch1] 5 times, (3tr, ch1, 2tr) in first ch sp, slst in third ch of beg ch to join, slst in next ch sp. (*twelve 3tr groups*)
Round 3: (Ch3, 2tr) in same ch sp, ch1, [3tr in next ch sp, ch1] 11 times, slst in third ch of beg ch to join. (*twelve 3tr groups*)
Round 4: Ch3 in first ch sp, [3tr in next ch sp, ch2] 11 times, 3tr in first ch sp, slst in third ch of beg ch to join, slst in next ch sp. (*twelve 3tr groups*)
Round 5: (Ch3, 2tr, ch1, 3tr) in same ch sp, ch2, 3tr in next ch sp, ch2, [(3tr, ch1, 3tr) in next ch sp, ch2, 3tr in next ch sp, ch2] 5 times, slst in third ch of beg ch to join. (*eighteen 3tr groups*)
Round 6: Ch3 in first ch sp, [3tr in next ch sp, ch2] 17 times, 2tr in first ch sp, slst in third ch of beg ch to join, slst in next ch sp. (*eighteen 3tr groups*)
Round 7: (Ch3, 3tr) in same ch sp, ch2, [4tr in next ch sp, ch2] 17 times, slst in third ch of beg ch to join. (*eighteen 4tr groups*)
Round 8: Ch3 in first ch sp, [4tr in next ch sp, ch2] 17 times, 3tr in first ch sp, slst in third ch of beg ch to join, slst in next ch sp. (*eighteen 4tr groups*)
Round 9: (Ch3, 1tr, ch1, 2tr) in same ch sp, ch2, [(2tr, ch1, 2tr) in next ch sp, ch2] 17 times, slst in third ch of beg ch to join. (*thirty-six 2tr groups*)
Round 10: Ch3 in first ch sp, ch2, [3tr in next ch-sp, ch2] 35 times, 2tr in first ch sp, slst in third ch of beg ch. (*thirty-six 3tr groups*)
Fasten off main colour, join contrasting colour in any ch sp.

BORDER
Round 11: Ch1, 1dc in same ch sp, ch4, [1dc in next ch-sp, ch4] 35 times, slst in first ch to join, slst into next ch sp. (*36 dc, thirty-six 4-ch sp*)
Round 12: (1dc, 1htr, 1tr, 1htr, 1dc) in each 4-ch sp around, slst in top of dc from prev round. (*36 petals*)
Fasten off.

COASTER

Using main colour, make a magic ring.
Round 1: Ch3 (counts as first tr throughout), 2tr in ring, ch1, [3tr in ring, ch1] 5 times, slst in third ch of beg ch to join. (*six 3tr groups*)
Work in ch sp between tr groups from prev rounds throughout.
Round 2: Ch3 in first ch sp, [(3tr, ch1, 3tr) in next ch sp, ch1] 5 times, (3tr, ch1, 2tr) in first ch sp, slst in third ch of beg ch to join, slst in next ch sp. (*twelve 3tr groups*)
Round 3: (Ch3, 2tr) in same ch sp, ch1, [3tr in next ch sp, ch1] 11 times, slst in third ch of beg ch to join. (*twelve 3tr groups*)

BORDER
Round 4: Ch1, 1dc in same ch sp, ch4, [1dc in next ch-sp, ch4] 11 times, slst in first ch to join, slst into next ch sp. (*12 dc, twelve 4-ch sp*)
Round 5: (1dc, 1htr, 1tr, 1htr, 1dc) in each 4-ch sp around, slst in top of dc from prev round. (*12 petals*)
Fasten off.

FINISHING
Sew in ends (see page 120).

SKILL RATING ● ○ ○

YARN AND MATERIALS
Knitcraft Cotton Blend DK (50% cotton, 50% acrylic) DK (light worsted) weight yarn, 215m (235yd) per 100g (3½oz) ball
  1 ball in each of:
  Hot Pink (1003)
  Red (1001)
  Coral (1007)
  Bright Blue (1005)
  Mustard (1001)
  Yellow (1008)
  Teal (1002)
  Lilac (1006)

HOOK AND EQUIPMENT
4mm (US size G/6) crochet hook
Yarn needle

FINISHED MEASUREMENTS
Approx 31cm (12½in) diameter

ABBREVIATIONS
See page 126.

Make this sweet caterpillar to keep your home warm and add a burst of colour to your décor. The pattern uses simple double crochet stitches to create the 3D shape, and is finished with cute face details and antennae.

caterpillar draught excluder

SKILL RATING ● ○ ○

YARN AND MATERIALS
Women's Institute Premium Acrylic Yarn (100% acrylic) DK (light worsted) weight yarn, 250m (273yd) per 100g (3½oz) ball
  1 ball in each of:
  Red 1015 (A)
  Orange 1002 (B)
  Yellow 1025 (C)
  Green 1001 (D)
  Soft Blue 1025 (E)
  Magenta 1031 (F)
  Soft Pink 1026 (G)
Small amount of black DK (light worsted) yarn
Pair of safety eyes
Fibre filling

HOOK AND EQUIPMENT
8mm (US size L/11) crochet hook
Yarn needle

FINISHED MEASUREMENTS
63cm (24¾in) long by 28cm (11in) circumference

ABBREVIATIONS
See page 126.

CATERPILLAR
Use three strands of each colour held together.
Using A, make a magic ring.
Round 1: 6dc in ring. *(6 dc)*
Round 2: 2dc in each st. *(12 dc)*
Round 3: [1dc, 2dc in next st] 6 times. *(18 dc)*
Round 4: [2dc, 2dc in next st] 6 times. *(24 dc)*
Round 5: [3dc, 2dc in next st] 6 times. *(30 dc)*
Insert safety eyes between Rounds 3 and 4, 10 sts apart.
Rounds 6-9: 1dc in each st.
Round 10: [3dc, dc2tog] 6 times. *(24 dc)*
Round 11: [2dc, dc2tog] 6 times. *(18 dc)*
Round 12: [1dc, dc2tog] 6 times. *(12 dc)*
Start to stuff with fibre filling.
Fasten off A, join B.
Rounds 13-22: Rep Rounds 3-12.
Cont to stuff with fibre filling.
Fasten off B, join C.
Rounds 23-32: Rep Rounds 3-12.
Cont to stuff with fibre filling.
Fasten off C, join D.
Rounds 33-42: Rep Rounds 3-12.
Cont to stuff with fibre filling.
Fasten off D, join E.
Rounds 43-52: Rep Rounds 3-12.
Cont to stuff with fibre filling.

Fasten off E, join F.
Rounds 53-62: Rep Rounds 3-12. Cont to stuff with fibre filling. Fasten off F, join G.
Rounds 63-72: Rep Rounds 3-12.
Round 73: [Dc2tog] 6 times. *(6 dc)* Finish stuffing, fasten off and sew gap closed.

ANTENNAE
Use a single strand of black yarn. Ch35.
Row 1: Slst in second ch from hook, 33slst. *(34 slst)*

FINISHING
Sew in all ends (see page 12).
Thread antennae strip through top of head, between Rounds 5 and 6, and sew in place.
Using a single strand of black yarn, sew mouth onto front of head.

Keep your books, magazines and TV remote close to hand with this pretty and practical design. If you've mastered the basics of crochet and want to expand your skills, this pattern is a great way of trying out granny squares, 3D bobble stitches and tassels.

granny square sofa tidy

SKILL RATING ● ● ●

YARN AND MATERIALS
Women's Institute Premium Acrylic Yarn (100% acrylic) DK (light worsted) weight yarn, 250m (273yd) per 100g (3½oz) ball
   1 ball in each of:
   Soft Blue 1025
   Orange 1002
   Green 1001
   Red 1015
   Yellow 1005 (A)
   Blue 1024 (B)
   Cream 1004 (C)
   Soft Pink 1026 (D)
20cm (8in) wide piece of card

HOOK AND EQUIPMENT
4mm (US size G/6) crochet hook
Yarn needle

FINISHED MEASUREMENTS
51cm (20in) long x 36cm (14in) wide

ABBREVIATIONS
See page 126.

SPECIAL ABBREVIATION
2trCL (two-treble cluster): yrh, insert hook in st, yrh, pull through (3 loops on hook), yrh, pull through first 2 loops on hook (2 loops on hook), yrh, insert hook in same st, yrh, pull through (4 loops on hook), yrh, pull through first 2 loops on hook (3 loops on hook), yrh, pull through all 3 loops on hook.

3trCL (three-treble cluster): yrh, insert hook in st, yrh, pull through (3 loops on hook), yrh, pull through first 2 loops on hook (2 loops on hook), yrh, insert hook in same st, yrh, pull through (4 loops on hook), yrh, pull through first 2 loops on hook (3 loops on hook), yrh, insert hook in same st, yrh, pull through (5 loops on hook), yrh, pull through first 2 loops on hook (4 loops on hook), yrh, pull through all 4 loops on hook.

Bobble: yrh, insert hook in st, yrh, pull through (3 loops on hook), yrh, pull through first 2 loops on hook (2 loops on hook), yrh, insert hook in same st, yrh, pull through (4 loops on hook), yrh, pull through first 2 loops on hook (3 loops on hook), yrh, insert hook in same st, yrh, pull through (5 loops on hook), yrh, pull through first 2 loops on hook (4 loops on hook), yrh, insert hook in same st, yrh, pull through (6 loops on hook), yrh, pull through first 2 loops on hook (5 loops on hook), yrh, insert hook in same st, yrh, pull through (7 loops on hook), yrh, pull through first 2 loops on hook (6 loops on hook), yrh, pull through all 6 loops on hook.

SOFA TIDY

SQUARES
(make 4 in assorted colours other than A, B, C or D)
Using first colour, make a magic ring.
Round 1: Ch3, 1tr in ring, (counts as one 2trCL), ch1, [2trCL, ch1] 7 times in ring, slst in first st. *(8 2trCL, 8 ch sps)*
Fasten off first colour, join second colour in any ch sp.
Round 2: Working in ch sps from prev round, ch3, 2tr in first ch sp (counts as one 3trCL), ch1, [3trCL, ch1] 7 times, slst in first st. *(8 3trCL, 8 ch sps)*
Fasten off second colour, join third colour in any ch sp.
Round 3: Working in ch sps from prev round, ch3 (counts as 1 tr), (2tr, ch2, 3tr) in first ch sp (corner), 3tr in next ch sp, *(3tr, ch2, 3tr) in next ch sp (corner), 3tr in next ch sp; rep from * twice, slst in first st. *(12 x 3tr groups, 4ch sps)*
Place 4 squares in a line and sew together using mattress stitch.

Top border
Join A in top RH corner of row of squares.
Row 1 (RS): Ch1 (does not count as a st throughout), 1dc in each st, ch sp and gap between 3tr groups along edge of squares to LH corner of last square, turn. *(52 dc)*
Rows 2 and 3: Ch1, 1htr in each st, turn.
Join B, do not fasten off A.
Carry yarn not in use within each st as you make it.
Row 4 (WS): Ch1, [3dc in A, Bobble in B] 12 times, 4dc in A, turn.
Fasten off B, do not fasten off A.
Rows 5 and 6: Ch1, 1htr in each st, turn.
Row 7: Ch1, 1dc in each st.
Fasten off A.

Main section
Rotate to work along opp side of squares. Join C in RH corner of first square.
Row 1 (RS): Ch1 (does not count as a st throughout), 1dc in each st, ch sp and gap between 3tr groups along edge of squares to LH corner of last square, turn. *(52 dc)*
Rows 2-61: Ch1, 52htr.
Fasten off C, join A.

Bottom border
Row 1 (WS): Ch1, 1dc in each st, turn. *(52 dc)*
Rows 2 and 3: Ch1, 1htr in each st, turn.
Join B, do not fasten off A.
Carry yarn not in use within each st as you make it.
Row 4 (RS, will get folded to WS): Ch1, [3dc in A, Bobble in B] 12 times, 4dc in A, turn.
Fasten off B, do not fasten off A.
Rows 5 and 6: Ch1, 1htr in each st, turn.
Fasten off A and sew in ends.

FINISHING

Fold top border of sofa tidy approximately a quarter up main section.
Join C in top corner.
Row 1: Ch1, 1dc in each row end of main body to folded section, 1dc in each row end through both layers to create the pocket.
Fasten off and sew in ends.
Rep on other side.

TASSELS
(make 2)
Wrap D around card approximately 20 times.
Tie all strands at tip with length of D yarn, leaving tail to sew to corners of sofa tidy.
Gently pull all strands from card and cut loops at opp end.
A third down from top, wrap a length of A four to six times around and knot securely.
Sew a tassel to each pocket bottom corner.

Made in beautiful vibrant colours, this wall tidy is ideal for storing anything from books and wrapping paper to clothes and toys. The flower petals add a unique detail to the traditional granny squares.

flower square wall tidy

SKILL RATING ●●○

YARN AND MATERIALS
Knitcraft Cotton Blend DK (50% cotton, 50% acrylic) DK (light worsted) weight yarn, 215m (235yd) per 100g (3½oz) ball
  1 ball in each of:
  Hot Pink 1003 (A)
  Yellow 1008 (B)
  Bright Blue 1005 (C)
  Red 1001 (D)
  Teal 1002 (E)
2 lengths of dowel, each 30.5cm (12in) long

HOOK AND EQUIPMENT
4mm (US size G/6) crochet hook
Yarn needle

FINISHED MEASUREMENTS
29cm (11½in) wide by 30cm (11¾in) tall when folded

ABBREVIATIONS
See page 126.

SPECIAL ABBREVIATION
Standing dc: Wrap new yarn around hook from the back twice. Insert hook into stitch, yrh and pull up a loop. Complete dc as normal.

WALL TIDY
SQUARES
(make 3)
Using A, make a magic ring.
Round 1: Ch4 (counts as 1tr, ch1), [1tr in ring, ch1] 11 times, slst in third ch of beg 4-ch to join. *(12 tr, twelve 1-ch sp)*
Fasten off A, join B with a standing dc in any ch sp.
Round 2: Ch2, [1dc in next 1-ch sp, ch2] 11 times, slst in first dc to join. *(12 dc, twelve 2-ch sp)*
Fasten off B, join C with a standing dc around BP of any dc from Round 2.
Round 3: Ch2, [1dc around BP of next dc, ch2] 11 times, slst in first dc to join. *(12 dc, twelve 2-ch sp)*
Round 4: Slst in next 2-ch sp, ch3 (counts as 1tr), (2tr, ch2, 3tr) in same sp, [2tr in next 2-ch sp] twice, *(3tr, ch2, 3tr) in next 2-ch sp, [2tr in next 2-ch sp] twice; rep from * twice, slst in first tr to join.
Fasten off C, join B in any corner sp from Round 4.
Round 5: (Ch 3, 2tr, ch2, 3tr) in corner ch sp, [3tr between next two tr groups] 3 times, *(3tr, ch2, 3tr) in corner ch sp, [3tr between next two tr groups] 3 times; rep from * twice, slst in first tr to join.
Fasten off B, join D in any 2-ch sp of Round 2.
Round 6: *(Slst, ch2, 2tr, ch2, slst) in 2-ch sp; rep from * 11 times, slst in first slst to join. *(12 petals)*
Fasten off D.
Place 3 squares in a line and sew together using mattress stitch (see page 121).
First channel
Working in tops of squares, join A in top RH corner ch sp.

Row 1: Ch3 (counts as 1tr), 1tr in same sp, 3tr in each sp between 3tr groups on top edge of squares and 3tr in each join between squares, 2tr in corner ch sp, ch2, turn. *(Fourteen 3tr groups, two 2tr groups)*
Rows 2-5: 1htr in each st to the end, ch2, turn. *(46 htr)*
Fasten off leaving a long tail.

Granny stripe section
Join A to opp side of squares in top RH corner ch sp.
Row 1: Ch3, 1tr in same sp, 3tr between each pair of tr groups, 2tr in last ch sp. *(Fourteen 3tr groups, two 2tr groups)*
Fasten off A. Join C.
Row 2: Ch3, 3tr between each pair of tr groups, 1tr in last tr. *(Fifteen 3tr groups, 2tr)*
Fasten off C. Join B.
Row 3: Repeat Row 1.
Fasten off B. Join D.
Row 4: Repeat Row 2.
Fasten off D, join E with RS facing.

Main section
Rows 5-44: Ch2 (counts as first htr), 1htr in each st to end, ch2, turn. *(47 htr)*
Row 45: Ch2 (counts as first htr), 1htr in each st to end.
Fasten off leaving a long tail.
Fold first channel section in A over to WS and sew edge to Row 1 to form a channel for one dowel. Fold four rows of main section over to WS and sew to create channel for second dowel.

Border
Join E to any row edge.
Round 1: Work dc along side edge evenly spaced across the row ends. Repeat for second edge.
Fasten off and sew in ends (see page 120).

HANGING CHAINS
Using E, make two lengths of 30ch and one length of 50ch.
Starting in the second st from hook, work 1slst in each ch. Fasten off leaving a long tail for each length to sew onto tidy.

FINISHING
Lay tidy flat with RS of squares facing down. Fold squares and striped section up over main section. Sew one end of a 30-ch length to end of first channel at one end and other end to end of second channel at matching end (see photograph for guidance). Repeat with second 30-ch length on other side. Sew ends of 50-ch length to opposite sides at top of second channel.

under the rainbow blanket

Get cosy with this showstopping blanket design. Each of the squares could be worked up when you have a spare evening. The pieces are then sewn together and a rainbow border is added for the finishing touch.

SKILL RATING ● ● ●

YARN AND MATERIALS
Women's Institute Premium Acrylic Yarn (100% acrylic) DK (light worsted) weight yarn, 250m (273yd) per 100g (3½oz) ball
  1 ball in each of:
  Yellow 1005 (A)
  Soft Blue 1025 (C)
  Green 1001 (D)
  Orange 1002 (E)
  Red 1024 (F)
  2 balls in each of:
  Soft Pink 1026 (B)
  Petrol 1029 (G)

HOOK AND EQUIPMENT
4mm (US size G/6) crochet hook
Yarn needle

FINISHED MEASUREMENTS
104cm (41½in) square

ABBREVIATIONS
See page 126.

SPECIAL ABBREVIATION
Picot: Ch3, slst in second ch from hook, slst in next ch.

SUNSHINE SQUARE
(make 4)
Using A, make a magic ring.
Round 1: Ch3 (counts as 1tr throughout), 11tr in ring, slst in top of beg 3-ch to join. *(12 tr)*
Round 2: Ch3, 1tr in same st, [2tr in next st] 11 times, slst in top of beg 3-ch to join. *(24 tr)*
Round 3: Ch3, 2tr in next st, [1tr, 2tr in next st] 11 times, slst in top of beg 3-ch to join. *(36 tr)*
Round 4: *SlstFLO, (1trFLO, picot, 1trFLO) in next st, slstFLO; rep from * 11 times, slst in beg slst to join. Fasten off A, join B in any unworked back loop from Round 4.
Round 5: Ch3, 1trBLO, 4htrBLO, 2trBLO, (2trBLO, ch2, 2trBLO) in next st (corner), *2trBLO, 4htrBLO, 2trBLO, (2trBLO, ch2, 2trBLO) in next st; rep from * twice more, slst in top ch of beg 3-ch to join. *(32 tr, 16 htr, four 2-ch sp)*
Round 6: Ch3, 1tr in each st and (2tr, ch2, 2tr) in each corner sp, slst in top of beg 3-ch to join. *(64 tr, four 2-ch sp)*
Round 7: Rep Round 6. *(80 tr, four 2-ch sp)*
Fasten off B, join C in corner sp.
Round 8: (Ch3, 2tr, ch2, 3tr) in same corner sp, [miss next 2 sts, 3tr in next st] 6 times, ** miss next 2 sts, (3tr, ch2, 3tr) in corner sp, [miss next 2 sts, 3tr in next st] 6 times; rep from ** twice more, miss last 2 sts, slst in top of beg 3-ch to join. *(96 tr, four 2-ch sp)*
Fasten off and sew in ends (see page 120).

RAINBOW SQUARE
(make 4)
Using B, make a magic ring.
Row 1: Ch3 (counts as 1tr throughout), 2tr in ring. *(3 tr)*
Fasten off B, join C.
Row 2: Ch3, turn, 1tr in same st, [2tr in next st] twice. *(6 tr)*
Fasten off C, join D.
Row 3: Ch3, turn, 2tr in next st, [1tr, 2tr in next st] twice. *(9 tr)*
Fasten off D, join A.
Row 4: Ch3, turn, 1tr, 2tr in next st, [2tr, 2tr in next st] twice. *(12 tr)*
Fasten off A, join E.
Row 5: Ch3, turn, 2tr, 2tr in next st, [3tr, 2tr in next st] twice. *(15 tr)*
Fasten off E, join F.
Row 6: Ch3, turn, 3tr, 2tr in next st, [4tr, 2tr in next st] twice. *(18 tr)*
Fasten off F, join B.
Row 7: Ch3, turn, 4tr, 2tr in next st, [5tr, 2tr in next st] twice. *(21 tr)*
Fasten off B, join C.
Row 8: Ch3, turn, 5tr, 2tr in next st, [6tr, 2tr in next st] twice. *(24 tr)*
Row 9: Ch1 (does not count as dc throughout), turn, 3dc, 3htr, 3tr, 2dtr, 2dtr in next st, ch2, 2dtr in next st, 2dtr, 3tr, 3htr, 3dc. *(26 sts, one 2-ch sp)*
Row 10: Ch1, turn, 4dc, 3htr, 3tr, 3dtr, (2dtr, ch2, 2dtr) in 2-ch sp, 3dtr, 3tr, 3htr, 4dc. *(30 sts, one 2-ch sp)*
Row 11: Ch3, turn, 1tr in same st, 1tr in each st to corner sp, (2tr, ch2, 2tr) in corner sp, 1tr in each st to last st, 2tr in last st. *(36 sts, one 2-ch sp)*

under the rainbow blanket

Row 12: Ch3, turn, 1tr in each st to corner sp, (2tr, ch2, 2tr) in corner sp, 1tr in each st to end. *(40 tr, one 2-ch sp)*
Fasten off C, join A in bottom right (RS facing) corner ch sp.
Row 13: (Ch3, 2tr, ch2, 3tr) in corner sp, *[miss 2 sts, 3tr in next st] 6 times, miss 2 sts, (3tr, ch2, 3tr) in next corner sp; rep from * once more, work six 3tr groups evenly spaced in row ends of next two sides of square working (3tr, ch2, 3tr) in corner sp, slst in top of beg 3-ch to join.
Fasten off and sew in ends.

RAIN CLOUD SQUARE
(make 2)
Using A, make a magic ring.
Round 1: Ch3 (counts as 1tr throughout), 2tr in ring, [ch2, 3tr] 3 times in ring, ch2, slst in top of beg 3-ch to join. *(12 tr, four 2-ch sp)*
Round 2: Ch3, 2tr, *(2tr, ch2, 2tr) in corner sp, 1tr in each st to next corner sp; rep from * twice more, (2tr, ch2, 2tr) in next corner sp, slst in top of beg 3-ch to join. *(28 tr, four 2-ch sp)*
Round 3: Ch3, 1tr in each st to next corner sp, *(2tr, ch2, 2tr) in corner sp, 1tr in each st to next corner; rep from * twice more, (2tr, ch2, 2tr) in last corner sp, 1tr in each st to end, slst in top of beg 3-ch to join. *(44 tr, four 2-ch sp)*
Round 4: Rep Round 3. *(60 tr, four 2-ch sp)*
Round 5: Rep Round 3. *(76 tr, four 2-ch sp)*
Round 6: Ch1, 1dc in each st to next corner sp, *(1dc, ch2) in corner sp, 1dc in each st to next corner; rep from * twice more, (1dc, ch2) in last corner sp, 1dc in each st to end, slst in first dc to join. *(80 sts, four 2-ch sp)*
Fasten off A, join D in any corner sp
Round 7: (Ch3, 2tr, ch2, 3tr) in corner sp, *[miss 2 sts, 3tr in next st] 6 times, miss 2 sts, (3tr, ch2, 3tr) in corner sp; rep from * twice more, [miss 2 sts, 3tr in next st] 6 times, miss 2 sts, slst in top of beg 3-ch to join.
Fasten off and sew in ends.

CLOUD
(make 2)
Using C, ch13.
Round 1: 1dc in second ch from hook, 10dc, 3dc in the last ch, working along opp side of foundation chain, 10dc, 2dc in last ch, slst in first dc to join. *(26 dc)*
Row 2: Ch1, miss first st, 4tr in next st, 8tr, 4tr in next st, slst in next st, turn. *(16 tr)*
Row 3: Slst in next 4 tr, miss next st, 6tr in next st, miss next st, slst in next st, miss next 2 sts, (4dtr, 4tr) in next st, miss next st, slst in next st.
Fasten off leaving a long tail to sew cloud to square.

RAINDROPS
(make 1 in each of B, D, E, F)
Make a magic ring.
Round 1: Ch1, 2dc in ring, ch3, 3dc in ring, slst in first dc. Fasten off, leaving a long tail to sew raindrops to square.

FLOWER SQUARE
(make 5)
Using E, make a magic ring.
Round 1: Ch3 (counts as 1tr throughout), 11tr in ring, slst in top of beg 3-ch to join. *(12 tr)*
Round 2: Ch3, 1tr in same st, [2tr in next st] 11 times, slst in top of beg 3-ch to join. *(24 tr)*
Fasten off E, join F between any 2 tr.
Round 3: Ch1, working between tr throughout, [1dc, ch4, miss 3tr] 8 times, slst in first dc to join.
Round 4: *(Slst , ch3, 3dtr, ch3, slst) in 4-ch sp, rep from * 7 times.
Fasten off F, join D into BLO of any tr from Round 2.
Round 5: Working into BLO of tr in Round 2, ch3, 2tr in next st, [1tr, 2tr in next st] 11 times, slst in top of beg 3-ch to join. *(36 sts)*
Round 6: Ch3, (1tr, ch2, 2tr) in same st, 1tr, 1htr, 4dc, 1htr, 1tr, *(2tr, ch2, 2tr) in next st, 1tr, 1htr, 4dc, 1htr, 1tr; rep from * twice, slst in top of beg 3-ch to join. *(48 sts, four 2-ch sps)*
Round 7: Ch3, 1tr in each st and (2tr, ch2, 2tr) into each 2-ch sp to end. *(64 sts)*
Round 8: Ch3, 1tr in each st and (2tr, ch2, 2tr) in each corner sp to end. *(80 sts)*
Fasten off D, join E in any corner sp.
Round 9: (Ch3, 2tr, ch2, 3tr) in corner sp, *[miss 2 sts, 3tr in next st] 6 times, miss 2 sts, (3tr, ch2, 3tr) in corner sp; rep from * twice more, [miss 2 sts, 3tr in next st] 6 times, miss 2 sts, slst in top of beg 3-ch to join.
Fasten off and sew in ends.

CONCENTRIC STRIPES SQUARE
(make 10)
Using C, make a magic ring.
Round 1: Ch3 (counts as 1tr throughout), 2tr in ring, [ch2, 3tr] 3 times in ring, ch2, slst in top of beg 3-ch to join. *(12 tr, four 2-ch sp)*
Fasten off C, join D.
Round 2: Ch3, 2tr, *(2tr, ch2, 2tr) in corner sp, 1tr in each st to next corner sp; rep from * twice more, (2tr, ch2, 2tr) in next corner sp, slst in top of beg 3-ch to join. *(28 tr, four 2-ch sp)*
Fasten off D, join A.
Round 3: Ch3, 1tr in each st to next corner sp, *(2tr, ch2, 2tr) in corner sp, 1tr in each st to next corner; rep from

* twice more, (2tr, ch2, 2tr) in last corner sp, 1tr in each st to end, slst in top of beg 3-ch to join. *(44 tr, four 2-ch sp)*
Fasten off A, join E.
Round 4: Rep Round 3. *(60 tr, four 2-ch sp)*
Fasten off E, join F.
Round 5: Rep Round 3. *(76 tr, four 2-ch sp)*
Fasten off F, join B.
Round 6: Ch1, 1dc in each st to next corner sp, *(1dc, ch2) in corner sp, 1dc in each st to next corner; rep from * twice more, (1dc, ch2) in last corner sp, 1dc in each st to end, slst in first dc to join. *(80 sts, four 2-ch sp)*
Round 7: (Ch3, 2tr, ch2, 3tr) in corner sp, *[miss 2 sts, 3tr in next st] 6 times, miss 2 sts, (3tr, ch2, 3tr) in corner sp; rep from * twice more, [miss 2 sts, 3tr in next st] 6 times, miss 2 sts, slst in top of beg 3-ch to join.
Fasten off and sew in ends.

BORDER TO EACH SQUARE
Join G in any corner sp.
Round 1: Ch3, (2tr, ch2, 3tr) in corner sp, [3tr between next two 3tr groups] 7 times, *(3tr, ch2, 3tr) in corner sp, [3tr between next two 3tr groups] 7 times; rep from * twice more, slst in top of beg 3-ch to join.
Fasten off.

FINISHING
Sew the cloud and the raindrops to the rain cloud square, following the photograph as a guide.
Lay out all squares in order, following the diagram as a guide. Using G, sew squares together using mattress stitch (see page 121) through the back loops only.
Main border
Worked in half treble over 7 rows. Work all rows in same way, changing colour at end of each row in following colour sequence: G, C, D, A, E, F, B.
Rows 1–7: Ch2 (counts as 1 htr), 1htr in each st around and (2htr, ch2, 2htr) in each corner sp.
Fasten off and sew in ends.

table runner

Create a unique table setting with this colourful and simple granny-square pattern. Made in variety of bright shades of durable cotton-blend yarn, this runner will protect your table from warm dishes and mugs.

SKILL RATING ● ○ ○

YARN AND MATERIALS
Knitcraft Cotton Blend DK (50% cotton, 50% acrylic) DK (light worsted) weight yarn, 215m (235yd) per 100g (3½oz) ball
 1 ball in each of:
 Bright Blue 1005 (A)
 Red 6230001001 (B)
 Mustard 1001 (C)
 Hot Pink 1003 (D)
 Teal 1002 (E)
 Yellow 1008 (F)
 Lilac 6230001006 (G)
 Coral 6230001007 (H)

HOOK AND EQUIPMENT
4mm (US size G/6) crochet hook
Yarn needle

FINISHED MEASUREMENTS
Each square: 10.5cm (4¼in) square
Runner: 150cm (59in) long

ABBREVIATIONS
See page 126.

NOTE
Either use the Join As You Go method (see page 122) in the spaces between 3-tr groups as you work Round 4 or sew together with mattress stitch (see page 121) afterwards.

SQUARE
(make 14 in A, 2 each in B, C, D, E, F, G, H)
Make a magic ring.
Round 1: Ch3 (counts as 1tr throughout), (2tr, ch2) in ring, [3tr, ch2] 3 times in ring, sl st in third ch of beg ch to join.
Round 2: Ch3, [(3tr, ch2, 3tr) in next 2-ch sp] 3 times, (3tr, ch2, 2tr) in last 2-ch sp, sl st in third ch of beg ch to join.
Round 3: Ch3, 2tr in first sp between two 3tr groups, *(3tr, ch2, 3tr) in next 2-ch sp (corner), 3tr in sp between next two 3tr groups; rep from * twice, (3tr, ch2, 3tr) in next 2-ch sp (corner), sl st in third ch of beg ch to join.
Round 4: Ch3, 3tr in sp between next two 3tr groups, *(3tr, 2ch, 3tr) in corner sp, [3tr in sp between next two 3tr groups] twice; rep from * twice, (3tr, 2ch, 3tr) in corner sp, 2tr in sp between next two 3tr groups, sl st in third ch of beg ch to join.

FINISHING
Arrange squares as you wish or use photo as guide.
Join squares together using relevant color.

BORDER
Join A to any corner.
Round 1: *(1dc, ch2, 2dc) in first corner ch sp of this side, 1dc in each st and each inner corner ch sp along this side, rep from * 3 times, sl st in first st to join. (29 sts on each short side, 197 sts on each long side)
Fasten off A, join C in any corner sp.
Round 2: *(1dc, ch2, 1dc) in corner sp, (ch3, miss 2 dc, 1dc) along this side to last 2 dc, ch3, miss 2 dc, rep from * 3 times, sl st in first st to join.
Fasten off C, join D in any corner sp.
Round 3: (2dc, ch1, 2dc) in each corner sp and 4dc in each ch sp from prev round, sl st in first st to join.
Fasten off and sew in ends (see page 120).

tissue box cover

Stitch up this fun geometric design to customise an ordinary tissue box. Deceptively easy to make, the pattern is worked up in half-treble stitches in two different yarn colours. A simple flower is crocheted and sewn onto the cover to finish.

SKILL RATING ● ● ○

YARN AND MATERIALS
Women's Institute Premium Acrylic Yarn (100% acrylic) DK (light worsted) weight yarn, 250m (273yd) per 100g (3½oz) ball
  1 ball in each of:
  White 1000 (A)
  Orange 1002 (B)
  Magenta 1031 (C)
  Soft Blue 1025 (D)
Tissue box 12cm (4¾in) square

HOOK AND EQUIPMENT
4mm (US size G/6) crochet hook
Yarn needle

FINISHED MEASUREMENTS
Approx 12cm (4¾in) square

ABBREVIATIONS
See page 126.

COVER SIDES
Using A, ch72, slst in first ch to form a ring.
Join B, carry yarn not in use throughout.
Round 1: Ch2, (does not count as a st throughout), [3htr in A, 3htr in B] 12 times, slst in first st to join. *(72 htr)*
Round 2: Rep Round 1.
Round 3: Ch2, [3htr in B, 3htr in A] 12 times, slst in first st to join.
Round 4: Rep Round 3.
Rounds 5-12: Rep Rounds 1-4 twice.
Fasten off and sew in ends (see page 120).

COVER TOP
Using B, ch19.
Row 1: 1htr in second ch from hook, 1htr in each ch to end, ch1, turn. *(18 htr)*
Rows 2-5: Ch2, (does not count as a st throughout), 1htr in each st to end, ch1, turn.
Row 6: Ch2, 6htr, fasten off, miss 6 sts, rejoin yarn, 1htr in last 6 sts, ch1, turn.
Row 7: Ch2, 6htr, ch6, 6htr, ch1, turn.
Row 8: Ch2, 6htr, 6htr in 6-ch sp, 6htr. *(18 htr)*
Rows 9-12: 1htr in each st to end, ch1, turn.
Fasten off leaving a long tail.

FLOWER
Using C, make a magic ring.
Round 1: 12tr into ring.
Fasten off C, join D.
Round 2: *(Slst, ch3, 2dtr, ch3, slst) in next st, slst in next st; rep from * 5 more times, slst in first slst to join.
Fasten off leaving a long tail to sew to tissue box.

FINISHING
Sew top into top edge of sides.
Sew flower onto one side of tissue box.

CHAPTER 2
Cute Accessories & Gifts

With a sweet bumble bee, a mini mushroom and bright flowers, these eye-catching bookmarks are perfect for using up colourful yarns. Each piece is quick to hook up, making this an ideal project to pick up when you have a spare moment during a busy day. One of these paired with a book would make a great gift.

bookmarks

SKILL RATING ● ● ●

YARN AND MATERIALS
Rico Ricorumi DK (100% cotton) DK (light worsted) weight yarn, 58m (64yd) per 25g (1oz) ball

For Mushroom and Star bookmark:
  1 ball in each of:
    Fuchsia 014 (A)
    White 001 (B)
    Yellow 006 (C)
    Green 049 (D)

For Flower and Leaf bookmark:
  1 ball in each of:
    Yellow 006 (C)
    Blue 032 (E)
    Green 049 (D)

For Bee and Flower bookmark:
  1 ball in each of:
    Yellow 006 (C)
    Chocolate 057 (F)
    White 001 (B)
    Green 049 (D)
    Red 028 (G)

Fabric glue if required

HOOK AND EQUIPMENT
3mm (US size C/2-D/3) crochet hook
Yarn needle

FINISHED MEASUREMENT
Mushroom and star bookmark: 31cm (12¼in)
Flower and leaf bookmark: 31cm (12¼in)
Bee and flower bookmark: 28cm (11in)

ABBREVIATIONS
See page 126.

SPECIAL ABBREVIATION
Picot: Ch3, slst in second ch from hook, slst in next ch.

MUSHROOM AND STAR BOOKMARK
MUSHROOM CAP
Using A, make a magic ring.
Round 1: 6dc in magic ring. *(6 dc)*
Round 2: [2dc in next st] 6 times. *(12 dc)*
Round 3: 1dc in each st around.
Round 4: [1dc, 2dc in next st] 6 times. *(18 dc)*
Rounds 5-8: 1dc in each st around.
Fasten off and sew in ends (see page 120).

SPOTS
(make 4)
Using B, make a magic ring.
Round 1: 6dc in magic ring. *(6 dc)*
Fasten off, leaving long tail to sew to cap.

STALK
Using B, make a magic ring.
Round 1: 6dc in magic ring. *(6 dc)*
Round 2: [2dc in next st] 6 times. *(12 dc)*
Rounds 3-12: 1dc in each st around.
Start to stuff with fibre filling.
Round 13: [Dc2tog] 6 times. *(6 dc)*
Fasten off and sew in ends.

cute accessories & gifts

STAR
(make 2)
Using C, make a magic ring.
Round 1: Ch3 (counts as 1tr), 9tr in magic ring. *(10 tr)*
Round 2: *Ch5, 1dc in second ch from hook, 1htr, 1tr, 1dtr (point), slst in each of next 2 tr; rep from * 4 more times, ending with slst in first tr.
Fasten off leaving long tail to sew flowers together.

CORD
Using D, ch51.
Round 1: Slst in second ch from hook, slst in each st to end. *(50 slst)*
Fasten off.

FINISHING
Sew or glue both sides of star together. Sew spots onto cap, then sew cap onto stalk. Sew one end of cord to bottom of mushroom and other end between points of star. Sew in all ends.

FLOWER AND LEAF BOOKMARK
FLOWER
(make 2)
Using C, make a magic ring.
Round 1: 6dc in magic ring. *(6 dc)*
Round 2: [2dc in next st] 6 times. *(12 dc)*
Fasten off C, join E.
Round 3: *(1dc, ch2, 2dtr, ch2, 1dc) in next dc, slst in next dc; rep from * 5 more times.
Fasten off leaving long tail to sew flowers together.

LEAF
(make 2)
Using D, ch9.
Round 1: 1dc in second ch from hook, 3htr, 3tr in next ch, 2htr, (2htr, picot, 2htr) in last ch, working along opp side of chain, 2htr, 3tr in next ch, 3htr, 1dc.
Fasten off leaving long tail to sew to cord.

CORD
Using D, ch51.
Round 1: Slst in second ch from hook, slst in each ch to end. *(50 slst)*
Fasten off.

FINISHING
Sew or glue flowers wrong sides together, sandwiching one end of cord between layers. Sew or glue leaves wrong sides together to other end of cord. Sew in all ends.

BEE AND FLOWER BOOKMARK
BEE BODY
Using C, make a magic ring.
Round 1: 6dc in magic ring. *(6 dc)*
Round 2: [2dc in next st] 6 times. *(12 dc)*
Round 3: 1dc in each st around.
Change to F, do not fasten off C.
Rounds 4 and 5: 1dc in each st around.
Change to C, do not fasten off F.
Rounds 6 and 7: 1dc in each st around.
Change to F, do not fasten off C.
Start to stuff with fibre filling.
Rounds 8 and 9: 1dc in each st around.
Change to C, fasten off F.
Round 10: 1dc in each st around.
Round 11: [Dc2tog] 6 times. *(6 dc)*
Finish stuffing, fasten off and sew closed, sew in ends.

WINGS
Using B, make a magic ring.
Round 1: (1dc, ch2, 2dtr, ch2, 1dc, ch2, 2dtr, ch2, slst) in magic ring.
Fasten off leaving long tail to sew to body.

FLOWER
(make 2)
Using D, make a magic ring.
Round 1: 5dc in magic ring. *(5 dc)*
Fasten off D, join G.
Round 2: [Ch3, 2tr, ch3, slst] 5 times in magic ring.
Fasten off and sew in ends.

FINISHING
Sew or glue flowers wrong sides together. Sew wings on back of bee. Sew one end of cord to bottom of bee and other between two petals of flower. Sew in all ends.

peg dolls

With cute mushroom hats, these little dolls would make lovely toys or decorations for a child's bedroom. You could also use them as colourful accents in your home, dotted around on shelves or on a table.

SKILL RATING ● ● ○

YARN AND MATERIALS
Rico Ricorumi DK (100% cotton) DK (light worsted) weight yarn, 58m (64yd) per 25g (1oz) ball
   1 ball in each of:
   Red 028 (A)
   White 001 (B)
   Candy Pink 012 (C)
   Berry 015 (dark pink) (D)
   Pea 077 (light green) (Vest 1)
   Burgundy 030 (Vest 1)
   Aqua 074 (blue) (Vest 2)
   Fox 025 (orange) (Vest 2)
   Nougat 056 (light brown) (Vest 3)
   Mustard 064 (Vest 3)

3 wooden peg dolls, 3.5cm (1¼in) diameter x 12cm (4¾in) tall

Fabric glue

HOOK AND EQUIPMENT
3mm (US size C/2-D/3) crochet hook
Yarn needle

FINISHED MEASUREMENTS
3.5cm (1¼in) diameter x 12cm (4¾in) tall

ABBREVIATIONS
See page 126.

LARGE MUSHROOM TOP
OUTER RED CAP
Using A, make a magic ring.
Round 1: 6dc in magic ring. *(6 dc)*
Round 2: [2dc in next st] 6 times. *(12 dc)*
Round 3: [1dc, 2dc in next st] 6 times. *(18 dc)*
Round 4: [2dc, 2dc in next st] 6 times. *(24 dc)*
Round 5: [3dc, 2dc in next st] 6 times. *(30 dc)*
Round 6: [4dc, 2dc in next st] 6 times. *(36 dc)*
Round 7: [5dc, 2dc in next st] 6 times. *(42 dc)*
Rounds 8 to 10: 1dc in each st around.
Do not fasten off.

INNER WHITE CAP
Using B, make a magic ring.
Rounds 1–7: Rep Rounds 1–7 of outer red cap.
Rounds 8 and 9: 1dc in each st around.
Fasten off and sew in ends.
Put B cap inside A cap, using A work 1dc through both parts of cap in each st around. *(42 dc)*
Fasten off and sew in ends (see page 120).

MEDIUM MUSHROOM TOP
OUTER PINK CAP
Using C, make a magic ring.
Round 1: 6dc in magic ring. *(6 dc)*
Round 2: 1dc in each st around.
Round 3: [2dc in next st] 6 times. *(12 dc)*
Round 4: 1dc in each st around.
Round 5: [1dc, 2dc in next st] 6 times. *(18 dc)*
Round 6: 1dc in each st around.
Round 7: [2dc, 2dc in next st] 6 times. *(24 dc)*
Round 8: 1dc in each st around.
Round 9: [3dc, 2dc in next st] 6 times. *(30 dc)*
Round 10: 1dc in each st around.
Round 11: [4dc, 2dc in next st] 6 times. *(36 dc)*
Round 12: 1dc in each st around.
Round 13: [5dc, 2dc in next st] 6 times. *(42 dc)*
Do not fasten off.

INNER WHITE CAP
Using B, make a magic ring.
Rounds 1-13: Rep Rounds 1-13 of outer pink cap.
Put B cap inside C cap, using C work 1dc through both parts of cap in each st around. *(42 dc)*

SMALL MUSHROOM TOP
OUTER BERRY CAP
Using D, make a magic ring.
Round 1: 6dc in magic ring. *(6 dc)*
Round 2: [2dc in next st] 6 times. *(12 dc)*
Round 3: [1dc, 2dc in next st] 6 times. *(18 dc)*
Round 4: [2dc, 2dc in next st] 6 times. *(24 dc)*
Round 5: [3dc, 2dc in next st] 6 times. *(30 dc)*
Rounds 6-8: 1dc in each st around.
Do not fasten off.

INNER WHITE CAP
Using B, make a magic ring.
Rounds 1-5: Rep Rounds 1-5 of outer berry cap.
Rounds 6 and 7: 1dc in each st around.
Fasten off and sew in ends.
Put B cap inside D cap, using D work 1dc through both parts of cap in each st around. *(30 dc)*

SMALL SPOTS
(make 13)
Using B, make a magic ring.
Round 1: 6dc in magic ring. *(6 dc)*
Fasten off leaving long end to sew to cap.

BIG SPOTS
(make 6)
Using B, make a magic ring.
Round 1: 6dc in magic ring. *(6 dc)*
Round 2: [2dc in next st] 6 times. *(12 dc)*
Fasten off leaving long end to sew to cap.

VEST
(make 3)
For Vest 1 change colour every 2 rows, for Vest 2 every 3 rows, for Vest 3 work half and half.
Using first colour, ch22, slst in first ch to form a ring. Work in continuous rounds.
Rounds 1-14: 1dc in each st around. *(22 dc)*
Fasten off and sew in ends.

FINISHING
Sew 3 big spots and 4 small spots on large mushroom cap.
Sew 2 big spots and 5 small spots on medium mushroom cap.
Sew 1 big spot and 4 small spots on small mushroom cap.
Glue each cap to a wooden doll.
Dress each wooden doll in a vest.

lavender heart

Embellished with a mini crocheted flower and leaves, this lavender heart would make a perfect gift or stocking filler. Put the heart on a coat hanger in a wardrobe or tuck it into a drawer to keep clothes smelling floral and fresh. Hanging up in a room, it doubles up as a beautiful decoration.

SKILL RATING ● ● ○

YARN AND MATERIALS
Women's Institute Premium Acrylic Yarn (100% acrylic) DK (light worsted) weight yarn, 250m (273yd) per 100g (3½oz) ball
  1 ball in each of:
  Red (A)
  Soft Pink (B)
  Yellow (C)
  Green (D)
  Soft Blue (E)
Lavender bag
Small amount of fibre filling

HOOK AND EQUIPMENT
4mm (US size G/6) hook
Yarn needle

FINISHED MEASUREMENTS
13cm (5in) wide x 11cm (4¼in) tall

ABBREVIATIONS
See page 126.

SPECIAL ABBREVIATION
PC (popcorn): work 6tr all in one st, remove live loop from hook, insert hook in top of first tr, place loop on hook and pull through.

HEART
FRONT AND BACK
(make 2)
Using A, make a magic ring.
Round 1: Ch2, 11tr in magic ring, slst in second ch of beg ch. *(11 tr, ch-2)*
Round 2: Ch2, [2tr in next tr] 11 times, slst in second ch of beg ch. *(22 tr, ch-2)*
Round 3: Ch2, [2tr in next tr, 1tr] 5 times, 2tr in next tr, 3tr in next tr, [1tr, 2tr in next tr] 5 times, slst in second ch of beg ch. *(35 tr, ch-2)*
Round 4: 1dc in top of ch-2, (1htr, 1tr) in next tr, [2tr in next tr] 5 times, 2tr, 2htr, 4dc, 1htr, 1tr, 3tr in next tr, 1tr, 1htr, 4dc, 2htr, 2tr, [2tr in next tr] 5 times, (1tr, 1htr) in next tr, 1dc, slst in first st. *(10 dc, 8 htr, 31 tr, 1 slst)*
Round 5: Slst in first dc, 1dc, 1htr, (1htr, 1tr) in next st, [2tr in next st] 6 times, 3tr, 2htr, 19dc, 2htr, 3tr, [2tr in next st] 6 times, (1tr, 1htr) in next st, 1htr, 1dc, slst, slst in first st *(21 dc, 8 htr, 32 tr, 3 slst)*
Fasten off and sew in ends (see page 120).

FLOWER
Using B, make a magic ring.
Round 1: Ch2 (counts as 1htr), 5htr, slst in second ch of beg ch. *(6 htr)*
Fasten off B, join C.
Round 2: PC in each sp between htr. *(6 PC)*
Fasten off C leaving long tail to sew to front of heart.

LEAF
(make 2)
Using D, ch7.
Round 1: 1dc in second ch from hook, 1htr, 2tr in next ch, 1htr, 1dc, 3dc in last ch, working along opp side of chain, 1dc, 1htr, 2tr in next ch, 1htr, 1dc, slst in first st.
Fasten off leaving long tail to sew to underside of flower.

HANGING LOOP
Using D, ch21, leaving a long tail.
Row 1: 1dc in second ch from hook, 1dc in each remaining ch. *(20 dc)*
Fasten off leaving long tail to sew to top of heart.

FINISHING
Put both hearts WS tog, join using E, with slst around both hearts (see page 122), placing dried lavender bag and small amount fibre filling inside before completing seam. *(64 slst)*
Sew flower and leaves to front of heart. Sew both ends of hanging loop to top centre of heart.

mug cosy

Keep your cup of tea or coffee warm with this sweet floral cosy. Quick to make, the pattern is made up of three simple granny squares which are sewn together and finished with a border, button loop and button. Why not stitch up a set of these in different colours for your mug collection?

SKILL RATING ● ○ ○

YARN AND MATERIALS
Rico Ricorumi DK (100% cotton) DK (light worsted) weight yarn, 58m (64yd) per 25g (1oz) ball
   1 ball in each of:
   Yellow 006 (A)
   Berry 015 (bright pink) (B)
   Green 049 (C)
Yellow button

HOOK AND EQUIPMENT
3.5mm (US size E/4) crochet hook
Yarn needle

FINISHED MEASUREMENTS
33cm (13in) circumference,
8.5cm (3¼in) tall

ABBREVIATIONS
See page 126.

SPECIAL ABBREVIATION
3trCL (three-treble cluster): yrh, insert hook in st, yrh, pull through (3 loops on hook), yrh, pull through first 2 loops on hook (2 loops on hook), yrh, insert hook in same st, yrh, pull through (4 loops on hook), yrh, pull through first 2 loops on hook (3 loops on hook), yrh, insert hook in same st, yrh, pull through (5 loops on hook), yrh, pull through first 2 loops on hook (4 loops on hook), yrh, pull through all 4 loops on hook.

COSY
SQUARES
(make 3)
Using A, make a magic ring.
Round 1: Working in magic ring, ch4 (counts as 1tr, ch1), [1tr, ch1] 7 times. *(8 tr, 8ch sps)*
Fasten off A, join B.
Round 2: Working in ch sps, [3trCL, ch2] 8 times.
Fasten off B, join C.
Round 3: Working in ch sps, ch3 (counts as 1tr), (2tr, ch2, 3tr) in same ch sp to make corner, 3dc in next ch sp, *(3tr, ch2, 3tr) in next ch sp to make corner, 3dc in next ch sp; rep from * 2 more times, slst in third ch of beg ch.
Round 4: Working in ch sps, ch3 (counts as 1tr), (2tr, ch2, 3tr) in same ch sp to make corner, 3dc in next 2 ch sps, *(3tr, ch2, 3tr) in corner ch sp, 3tr in next 2 ch sps; rep from * 2 more times, slst in third ch of beg ch.
Fasten off.

FINISHING
Sew squares together into a strip, then work 1dc in each st around, working 3dc in each corner.
Join last two sides together for 1cm (⅜in) up from bottom to make a ring, leaving rest of sides open above.
At top of opening, sew on button.
Button loop
Join C on side opposite button, ch11.
Row 1: Slst in second ch from hook, 9slst to end.
Fasten off leaving a long tail to sew other end of chain down to make button loop.

fridge magnets

This is a fun and simple project to start with if you are new to crochet. Made in brightly coloured cotton yarn, the mini crocheted pieces make super-cute magnets for your fridge or you could even sew them onto a bag or jacket.

SKILL RATING ● ○ ○

YARN AND MATERIALS
Rico Ricorumi DK (100% cotton) DK (light worsted) weight yarn, 58m (64yd) per 25g (1oz) ball
1 ball in each of:
Sky Blue 031 (A)
Green 049 (B)
Yellow 006 (C)
Orange 027 (D)
Red 028 (E)
Fuchsia 014 (F)
Tangerine 026 (G)
White 001 (H)

5 small round magnets

HOOK AND EQUIPMENT
3.5mm (US size E/4) crochet hook
Yarn needle
Fabric glue

FINISHED MEASUREMENTS
Rainbow: 7cm (2¾in) across
Sunshine: 8cm (3¼in) across
Flower: 6.5cm (2½in) across
Strawberry: 4.5cm (1¾in) across
Mushroom: 6.5cm (2½in) across

ABBREVIATIONS
See page 126.

SPECIAL ABBREVIATION
Picot: Ch3, slst in second ch from hook, slst in next ch.

RAINBOW

Using A, ch4.
Row 1: 1dc in second ch from hook, 1dc, 3dc in last ch, working along opp side of chain, 2dc. *(7 sts)*
Fasten off A, join B in first dc of Row 1.
Row 2: Ch1 (does not count as st throughout), 2dc, [2dc in next st] 3 times, 2dc. *(10 sts)*
Fasten off B, join C in first dc of Row 2.
Row 3: Ch1, 2dc, [1dc, 2dc in next st] 3 times, 2dc. *(13 sts)*
Fasten off C, join D in first dc of Row 3.
Row 4: Ch1, 2dc, [2dc, 2dc in next st] 3 times, 2dc. *(16 sts)*
Fasten off D, join E in first dc of Row 4.
Row 5: Ch1, 2dc, [3dc, 2dc in next st] 3 times, 2dc. *(19 sts)*
Fasten off E, join F in first dc of Row 5.
Row 6: Ch1, 2dc, [4dc, 2dc in next st] 3 times, 2dc. *(22 sts)*
Fasten off.

SUNSHINE

Using C, make a magic ring.
Round 1: 6dc in magic ring. *(6 sts)*
Round 2: [2dc in next st] 6 times. *(12 sts)*
Round 3: [1dc, 2dc in next st] 6 times. *(18 sts)*
Round 4: [2dc, 2dc in next st] 6 times. *(24 sts)*
Round 5: [3dc, 2dc in next st] 6 times. *(30 sts)*
Fasten off C, join G to any st.
Round 6: *(1dc, 1tr, picot) in next st, (1tr, 1dc) in next st; rep from * 14 more times.
Fasten off.

cute accessories & gifts

MUSHROOM

Using E, make a magic ring.
Row 1: 3dc in magic ring, ch1, turn. *(3 sts)*
Row 2: [2dc in next st] 3 times, ch1, turn. *(6 sts)*
Row 3: [1dc, 2dc in next st] 3 times, ch1, turn. *(9 sts)*
Row 4: [2dc, 2dc in next st] 3 times, ch1, turn. *(12 sts)*
Row 5: [3dc, 2dc in next st] 3 times, ch1, turn. *(15 sts)*
Row 6: 1dc in each st.
Fasten off.

STALK

Using H, ch4.
Row 1: 1dc in second ch from hook, 1dc, 3dc in last ch, working along opp side of chain, 2dc, turn. *(7 sts)*
Row 2: Ch1 (does not count as st), 2dc, [2dc in next st] 3 times, 2dc, turn. *(10 sts)*
Fasten off.

SPOT

(make 3)
Using H, make a magic ring.
Round 1: 6dc in magic ring. *(6 sts)*
Fasten off.

FINISHING

Sew in ends (see page 120) on Rainbow, Sunshine and Flower and glue a magnetic disc to back of each.
For Strawberry, sew on stalk, sew in ends and glue a magnetic disc to back.
For Mushroom, sew spots to cap, sew stalk to cap, then sew in ends. Glue a magnetic disc to back.

FLOWER

Using F, make a magic ring.
Round 1: 6dc in magic ring. *(6 sts)*
Round 2: [2dc in next st] 6 times. *(12 sts)*
Round 3: [1dc, 2dc in next st] 6 times. *(18 dc)*
Fasten off F, join D to any st.
Round 4: *(Slst, 1tr, 1dtr) in next st, (1dtr, 1tr, slst) in next st, slst; rep from * 5 more times.
Fasten off.

STRAWBERRY

Using E, make a magic ring.
Round 1: Ch3 (counts as first tr), 11tr in magic ring. *(12 sts)*
Round 2: (1htr, 1tr) in first st, 3tr in next st, 2htr, 3htr in next st, 2htr, 3tr in next st, (1tr, 1htr) in next st, 1dc, slst, 1dc. *(20 sts)*
Fasten off.

STALK

Using B.
Row 1: [Ch3, 1dc in second ch from hook, 1dc] 3 times.
Fasten off.

Coasters are always useful for any home, and this playful set would make a lovely gift. The spots on the ladybird's wings are crocheted separately and then stitched on. You could make several of the flower designs with different colours for the petals.

ladybird and flower coasters

SKILL RATING ●○○

YARN AND MATERIALS
Rico Ricorumi DK (100% cotton) DK (light worsted) weight yarn, 58m (64yd) per 25g (1oz) ball

For the Ladybird coasters
  1 ball in each of:
    Red 028 (A)
    Black 060 (B)

For the Flower coasters
  1 ball in each of:
    Yellow 006 (C)
    Orchid 016 (pink) (D)

HOOK AND EQUIPMENT
3.5mm (US size E/4) crochet hook
Yarn needle

FINISHED MEASUREMENTS
Ladybird coaster: 12cm (4¾in) across
Flower coaster: 13cm (5in) across

ABBREVIATIONS
See page 126.

LADYBIRD
BODY
Using A, make a magic ring.
Round 1: 6dc in magic ring. *(6 sts)*
Round 2: [2dc in next st] 6 times. *(12 sts)*
Round 3: [1dc, 2dc in next st] 6 times. *(18 sts)*
Round 4: [2dc, 2dc in next st] 6 times. *(24 sts)*
Round 5: [3dc, 2dc in next st] 6 times. *(30 sts)*
Round 6: [4dc, 2dc in next st] 6 times. *(36 sts)*
Round 7: [5dc, 2dc in next st] 6 times. *(42 sts)*
Round 8: [6dc, 2dc in next st] 6 times. *(48 sts)*
Round 9: [7dc, 2dc in next st] 6 times. *(54 sts)*
Round 10: [8dc, 2dc in next st] 6 times. *(60 sts)*
Round 11: [9dc, 2dc in next st] 6 times. *(66 sts)*
Round 12: [10dc, 2dc in next st] 6 times. *(72 sts)*
Fasten off A and join B.
Round 13: Slst in each st around, then slst across diameter over each round to create line to divide wings.
Fasten off and sew in ends (see page 120).

HEAD
Using B, make a magic ring.
Row 1: 3dc in magic ring, ch1, turn. *(3 sts)*
Row 2: [2dc in next st] 3 times, ch1, turn. *(6 sts)*
Row 3: [1dc, 2dc in next st] 3 times, ch1, turn. *(9 sts)*
Row 4: [2dc, 2dc in next st] 3 times, ch1, turn. *(12 sts)*
Row 5: [3dc, 2dc in next st] 3 times. *(15 sts)*
Fasten off and sew in ends.

SPOTS
(make 6)
Using B, make a magic ring.
Round 1: 6dc in magic ring. *(6 sts)*
Round 2: [2dc in next st] 6 times. *(12 sts)*
Fasten off.

FLOWER
Using C, make a magic ring.
Round 1: 6dc in magic ring. *(6 sts)*
Round 2: [2dc in next st] 6 times. *(12 sts)*
Round 3: [1dc, 2dc in next st] 6 times. *(18 sts)*
Round 4: [2dc, 2dc in next st] 6 times. *(24 sts)*
Round 5: [3dc, 2dc in next st] 6 times. *(30 sts)*
Round 6: [4dc, 2dc in next st] 6 times. *(36 sts)*
Round 7: [5dc, 2dc in next st] 6 times. *(42 sts)*
Round 8: [6dc, 2dc in next st] 6 times. *(48 sts)*
Round 9: [7dc, 2dc in next st] 6 times. *(54 sts)*
Round 10: [8dc, 2dc in next st] 6 times. *(60 sts)*
Fasten off C and join D.
Round 11: *Slst, (ch3, 1dtr) in next st, 2dtr in next st, (1dtr, ch3, slst) in next st; rep from * 14 more times to create 15 petals.

FINISHING
Sew spots onto ladybird.

This adorable hot water bottle cover is sure to bring a smile to a loved one's face. The main cover is made up of simple blocks of colour, and the door and windows are crocheted separately and sewn on. Window boxes complete with tiny flowers are added to finish.

little house hot water bottle cover

SKILL RATING ● ● ○

YARN AND MATERIALS
Women's Institute Premium Acrylic Yarn (100% acrylic) DK (light worsted) weight yarn, 250m (273yd)

1 ball in each of:
Soft Blue 1025 (A)
Yellow 1005 (B)
Green 1001 (C)
Red 1015 (D)
Blue 1024 (E)
White 1000 (F)

50cm (20in) length of elastic
Hot water bottle 17cm (6¾in) wide

HOOK AND EQUIPMENT
4mm (US size G/6) crochet hook
Yarn needle

FINISHED MEASUREMENTS
18cm (7in) wide by 33cm (13in) tall with bottom folded inside

ABBREVIATIONS
See page 126.

COVER
Using A, ch60, slst in first ch to form a ring.
Work in continuous rounds throughout.
House section
Rounds 1-34: 1dc in each st around. *(60 sts)*
Fasten off A, join B.
Roof section
Round 35: 1dc in each st around.
Work in BLO for all foll rounds.
Round 36: 1dc in each st around.
Round 37: 14dc, [dc2tog], 28dc, [dc2tog], 14dc. *(58 sts)*
Round 38: 13dc, [dc2tog], 28dc, [dc2tog], 13dc. *(56 sts)*
Round 39: 13dc, [dc2tog], 26dc, [dc2tog], 13dc. *(54 sts)*
Round 40: 12dc, [dc2tog], 26dc, [dc2tog], 12dc. *(52 sts)*
Round 41: 12dc, [dc2tog], 24dc, [dc2tog], 12dc. *(50 sts)*
Round 42: 11dc, [dc2tog], 24dc, [dc2tog], 11dc. *(48 sts)*
Round 43: 11dc, [dc2tog], 22dc, [dc2tog], 11dc. *(46 sts)*
Round 44: 10dc, [dc2tog], 22dc, [dc2tog], 10dc. *(44 sts)*
Round 45: 10dc, [dc2tog], 20dc, [dc2tog], 10dc. *(42 sts)*
Round 46: 9dc, [dc2tog], 20dc, [dc2tog], 9dc. *(40 sts)*
Round 47: Work 1dc in each st around.
Fasten off leaving a long tail to sew top of roof shut.

Grass section
Join C to Round 1.
Round 1: 1dc in each foundation ch around. *(60 sts)*
Round 2: [1dc, 1tr] 30 times.
Round 3: [1tr, 1dc] 30 times.
Rounds 4-7: Rep Rounds 2 and 3 twice.
Round 8: 1dc in each st around.
Round 9: 1dcBLO in each st around.
Rounds 10-15: 1dc in each st around.
Tie ends of elastic together to form a loop slightly smaller than diameter of water bottle cover.
Round 16: Working over elastic, 1dc in each st around.
Fasten off and sew in ends.

DOOR
Using D, ch5.
Row 1: 1dc in second ch from hook, 3dc, ch1, turn. *(4 sts)*
Rows 2-6: 1dc in each st to end, ch1, turn.
Edging
Round 7: 1dc in each st or row end around all sides of door, working 1 extra dc in each corner sp. *(24 sts)*
Fasten off leaving a long tail to sew door to house.

DOOR HANDLE
Using B, make a magic ring.
Round 1: 4dc in magic ring, slst in first dc.
Fasten off leaving a long tail to sew to door.

WINDOW
(make 4)
Using E, ch5.
Row 1: 1dc in second ch from hook, 3dc, ch1, turn. *(4 sts)*
Rows 2-4: 1dc in each st to end, ch1, turn.
Fasten off E, join F.
Round 5: 1dc in each st or row end around all sides of window, working 1 extra dc in each corner sp. *(20 sts)*
Fasten off leaving a long tail to sew window details and to sew window to house.

WINDOW BOX
(make 4)
Using B, ch7.
Row 1: 1dc in second ch from hook, 5dc, ch1, turn. *(6 sts)*
Fasten off leaving a long tail to sew to lower part of window.

FINISHING
Sew top of roof closed.
Sew door in middle at base of house. Sew on door handle.
Sew on windows and use yarn end in F to sew across middle horizontally and vertically for window bars.
Sew a window box below each window. Using D, make 4 to 5 French knots (see page 126) per window box for flowers. Using C, sew 10 to 12 straight stitches per window box for leaves.
Fold Rounds 10 to 16 of grass section inside and water bottle will sit inside neatly.

pencil toppers

Make your stationery stand out with these cute and colourful pencil toppers. If you're a beginner, these designs are a great way to practise your techniques on small-scale projects. A set of these toppers with colourful pencils would make a lovely gift for a child.

SKILL RATING ● ○ ○

YARN AND MATERIALS
Rico Ricorumi DK (100% cotton) DK (light worsted) weight yarn, 58m (64yd) per 25g (1oz) ball

For Mushroom Pencil Holder:
1 ball in each of:
White 001 (A)
Orchid 016 (B)

For Sunshine Pencil Holder:
1 ball in each of:
Tangerine 026 (C)
Yellow 006 (D)

For Flower Pencil Holder:
1 ball in each of:
Pistachio 047 (E)
Fuchsia 014 (F)
Sky Blue 031 (G)

Small amount of fibre filling

HOOK AND EQUIPMENT
3.5mm (US size E/4) crochet hook
Yarn needle

FINISHED MEASUREMENTS
Mushroom pencil holder: 7.5cm (3in)
Sunshine pencil holder: 9cm (3½in)
Flower pencil holder: 8.5cm (3¼in)

ABBREVIATIONS
See page 126.

SPECIAL ABBREVIATION
Picot: Ch3, slst in second ch from hook, slst in next ch.

MUSHROOM
PENCIL HOLDER
Using A, make a magic ring.
Round 1: 6dc in magic ring. *(6 sts)*
Rounds 2–16: 1dc in each st around.
Fasten off.

CAP
Using B, make a magic ring.
Round 1: 6dc in magic ring. *(6 sts)*
Round 2: [2dc in next st] 6 times. *(12 sts)*
Round 3: [1dc, 2dc in next st] 6 times. *(18 dc)*
Rounds 4–8: 1dc in each st around. *(18 sts)*
Fasten off.

FINISHING
Using A, evenly stitch eight French knots (see page 126) around cap.
Sew in ends and sew cap to stalk.

SUNSHINE
PENCIL HOLDER
Using C, make a magic ring.
Round 1: 6dc in magic ring. *(6 sts)*
Rounds 2–10: 1dc in each st around.
Fasten off.

SUN

Using D, make a magic ring.
Round 1: 6dc in magic ring. *(6 sts)*
Round 2: [2dc in next st] 6 times. *(12 sts)*
Round 3: [1dc, 2dc in next st] 6 times. *(18 dc)*
Round 4: [2dc, 2dc in next st] 6 times. *(24 dc)*
Fasten off and make a second circle in D, following Rounds 1 to 4.

Sun rays

Place one circle on top of other, with RS facing out, and join using C as follows, stuffing as you go.
Round 5: [Slst, picot, slst] 12 times.
Fasten off.

FINISHING

Sew both parts of pencil topper together and sew in ends (see page 120).

FLOWER

PENCIL HOLDER

Using E, make a magic ring.
Round 1: 6dc in magic ring. *(6 sts)*
Rounds 2–10: 1dc in each st around.
Fasten off.

FLOWER

Using F, make a magic ring.
Round 1: 6dc in magic ring. *(6 sts)*
Round 2: [2dc in next st] 6 times. *(12 sts)*
Fasten off and make a second circle in F, following Rounds 1 and 2.
Place one circle on top of other, with RS facing out, and join using G as follows.
Round 3: *(Slst, ch2, 1tr) in next st, (1tr, ch2, slst) in next st; rep from * 5 more times.
Fasten off.

FINISHING

Sew both parts of pencil topper together and sew in ends.

Add a cute focal point to your bookshelf with these quirky gnome characters. The 3D shapes are made with simple double crochet stitches, and each gnome is finished with a popcorn-stitch nose and brightly coloured eyes. Why not try using different yarns to make stripy outfits for Mr and Mrs Gnome?

gnome sweet gnome bookends

SKILL RATING ●●○

YARN AND MATERIALS
Rico Ricorumi DK (100% cotton) DK (light worsted) weight yarn, 58m (64yd) per 25g (1oz) ball

1 ball in each of:
Red 028 (A)
Green 044 (B)
Beige 055 (C)
White 001 (D)
Pastel Yellow 062 (E)
Tangerine 026 (F)
Sky Blue 031 (G)
Black (H)

2 pairs of 8mm (⅓in) blue or green safety eyes

Fibre filling
Wooden bookends
Glue

HOOK AND EQUIPMENT
3.5mm (US size E/4) crochet hook
Yarn needle

FINISHED MEASUREMENTS
Each gnome on a mushroom approx. 26cm (10¼in) tall

ABBREVIATIONS
See page 126.

SPECIAL ABBREVIATION
PC (popcorn): work 6tr all in one st, remove live loop from hook, insert hook in top of first tr, place loop on hook and pull through.

NOTE
Both gnomes are made in the same way, with a hat, head, body, legs and arms.

If you don't want to use wooden bookends, weight the base of the mushrooms before adding fibre filling and use as bookends without the wooden part.

72 cute accessories & gifts

GNOME

HAT
(make 1 in A, 1 in B)
Make a magic ring.
Round 1: 6dc in magic ring. *(6 sts)*
Round 2: 1dc in each st.
Round 3: [1dc, 2dc in next st] 3 times. *(9 sts)*
Round 4: 1dc in each st.
Round 5: [2dc, 2dc in next st] 3 times. *(12 sts)*
Round 6: 1dc in each st.
Round 7: [3dc, 2dc in next st] 3 times. *(15 sts)*
Round 8: 1dc in each st.
Round 9: [4dc, 2dc in next st] 3 times. *(18 sts)*
Round 10: 1dc in each st.
Round 11: [5dc, 2dc in next st] 3 times. *(21 sts)*
Round 12: 1dc in each st.
Round 13: [6dc, 2dc in next st] 3 times. *(24 sts)*
Round 14: 1dc in each st.
Round 15: [7dc, 2dc in next st] 3 times. *(27 sts)*
Round 16: 1dc in each st.
Fasten off leaving a long tail to sew to head.

HEAD
(make 2)
Using C, make a magic ring.
Round 1: 6dc in magic ring. *(6 sts)*
Round 2: [2dc in next st] 6 times. *(12 sts)*
Round 3: [1dc, 2dc in next st] 6 times. *(18 sts)*
Round 4: [2dc, 2dc in next st] 6 times. *(24 sts)*
Rounds 5 and 6: 1dc in each st around.
Round 7: 11dc, PC, 12dc.
Rounds 8 and 9: 1dc in each st around. *(24 sts)*
Insert safety eyes between Rounds 8 and 9, either side of nose, 5 sts apart.
Round 10: [2dc, dc2tog] 6 times. *(18 sts)*
Start to stuff with fibre filling.
Round 11: [1dc, dc2tog] 6 times. *(12 sts)*
Round 12: [dc2tog] 6 times. *(6 sts)*
Fasten off and sew gap closed.

MR GNOME'S BEARD
Using D, make a magic ring.
Row 1: 3dc in magic ring, ch1, turn. *(3 sts)*
Row 2: [2dc in next st] 3 times, ch1, turn. *(6 sts)*
Row 3: [1dc, 2dc in next st] 3 times, ch1, turn. *(9 sts)*
Row 4: [2dc, 2dc in next st] 3 times, ch1, turn. *(12 sts)*
Row 5: [3dc, 2dc in next st] 3 times, ch1, turn. *(15 sts)*
Row 6: [4dc, 2dc in next st] 3 times. *(18 sts)*
Fasten off leaving a long tail to sew to face.

MRS GNOME'S HAIR
Using E, make a magic ring.
Round 1: 6dc in magic ring. *(6 sts)*
Round 2: [2dc in next st] 6 times. *(12 sts)*
Round 3: [1dc, 2dc in next st] 6 times. *(18 sts)*
Round 4: [2dc, 2dc in next st] 6 times. *(24 sts)*
Round 5: [3dc, 2dc in next st] 6 times. *(30 sts)*
Round 6: 14dc, [ch15, slst into the second ch, sl st in next 13 ch, sl st in next st from Round 5] 16 times, slst into the first st.
Fasten off, leaving a long tail to sew to Mrs Gnome's head.

BODY
(make 2)
Using F for Mr Gnome and G for Mrs Gnome, make a magic ring.

gnome sweet gnome bookends

Round 1: 6dc in magic ring. *(6 sts)*
Round 2: [2dc in next st] 6 times. *(12 sts)*
Round 3: [1dc, 2dc in next st] 6 times. *(18 sts)*
Round 4: [2dc, 2dc in next st] 6 times. *(24 sts)*
Round 5: [3dc, 2dc in next st] 6 times. *(30 sts)*
Rounds 6-9: 1dc in each st around.
Change to B for Mr Gnome only.
Round 10: 1dcBLO in each st around.
Rounds 11 and 12: 1dc in each st around.
Round 13: [3dc, dc2tog] 6 times. *(24 sts)*
Round 14: [2dc, dc2tog] 6 times. *(18 sts)*
Start to stuff with fibre filling.
Round 15: [1dc, dc2tog] 6 times. *(12 sts)*
Round 16: [Dc2tog] 6 times. *(6 sts)*
Fasten off and sew gap closed.

MRS GNOME'S SKIRT
Join G to missed FLs of Round 10 of Mrs Gnome's body.
Round 1: [4dc, 2dc in next st] 6 times. *(36 sts)*
Rounds 2-9: 1dc in each st around.
Fasten off and sew in the ends.

ARM/LEG
(make 4 in C for arms, 4 in H for legs)
Make a magic ring.
Round 1: 6dc in magic ring. *(6 sts)*
Round 2: [1dc, 2dc in next st] 3 times. *(9 sts)*
Round 3: 1dc in each st around.
Start to stuff with fibre filling.
Round 4: [1dc, dc2tog] 3 times. *(6 sts)*
Arms
Change to F for Mr Gnome, change to G for Mrs Gnome.
Legs
Change to B for Mr Gnome, work 2 rounds A, 2 rounds D alternately for Mrs Gnome.
Rounds 5-12: 1dc in each st around.
Fasten off leaving a long tail to sew to body.

MUSHROOM
STALK
Using D, make a magic ring.
Round 1: 6dc in magic ring. *(6 sts)*
Round 2: [2dc in next st] 6 times. *(12 sts)*
Round 3: [1dc, 2dc in next st] 6 times. *(18 sts)*
Round 4: [2dc, 2dc in next st] 6 times. *(24 sts)*
Round 5: [3dc, 2dc in next st] 6 times. *(30 sts)*
Round 6: [4dc, 2dc in next st] 6 times. *(36 sts)*
Round 7: 1dcBLO in each st around.
Rounds 8-15: 1dc in each st around.
Round 16: [5dc, 2dc in next st] 6 times. *(42 sts)*
Round 17: [6dc, 2dc in next st] 6 times. *(48 sts)*
Round 18: [7dc, 2dc in next st] 6 times. *(54 sts)*
Round 19: [8dc, 2dc in next st] 6 times. *(60 sts)*
Fasten off and sew in the ends.

CAP
(make 1 in A, 1 in F)
Make a magic ring.
Round 1: 6dc in magic ring. *(6 sts)*
Round 2: [2dc in next st] 6 times. *(12 sts)*
Round 3: [1dc, 2dc in next st] 6 times. *(18 sts)*
Round 4: [2dc, 2dc in next st] 6 times. *(24 sts)*
Round 5: [3dc, 2dc in next st] 6 times. *(30 sts)*
Round 6: [4dc, 2dc in next st] 6 times. *(36 sts)*
Round **7:** [5dc, 2dc in next st] 6 times. *(42 sts)*
Round 8: [6dc, 2dc in next st] 6 times. *(48 sts)*
Round 9: [7dc, 2dc in next st] 6 times. *(54 sts)*
Round 10: [8dc, 2dc in next st] 6 times. *(60 sts)*
Rounds 11–13: 1dc in each st around.
Place cap on stalk.
Round 14: 1dc in each st around working in both cap and stalk to join, at roughly halfway around, start to stuff with fibre filling and cont to stuff until closed.

SMALL SPOTS
(make 6)
Using D, make a magic ring.
Round 1: 6dc in magic ring. *(6 sts)*
Fasten off leaving a long tail to sew to cap.

LARGE SPOTS
(make 4)
Using D, make a magic ring.
Round 1: 6dc in magic ring. *(6 sts)*
Round 2: [2dc in next st] 6 times. *(12 sts)*
Fasten off leaving a long tail to sew to cap.

FINISHING
Sew hair to Mrs Gnome's head. Sew cap onto each head, sew head to body. Sew on arms and legs. Sew beard to Mr Gnome's face and sew three small and two large spots to each mushroom cap, then sew a gnome sitting on top.
Glue each assembled gnome and mushroom onto a wooden bookend.

Super-quick to hook up and made in durable cotton yarn, this sweet keyring will help you find your keys easily. This project only needs a small amount of yarn, so it's perfect for using up scraps leftover from other projects. One of these would make a lovely housewarming gift.

mushroom home keyring

SKILL RATING ●●○

YARN AND MATERIALS
Rico Ricorumi DK (100% cotton) DK (light worsted) weight yarn, 58m (64yd) per 25g (1oz) ball

  1 ball in each of:
  Tangerine 026 (A)
  White 001 (B)
  Beige 055 (C)
  Sky Blue 031 (D)
  Green 049 (E)

Split ring

HOOK AND EQUIPMENT
3.5mm (US size E/4) crochet hook

Yarn needle

FINISHED MEASUREMENTS
Mushroom: 7cm (2¾in) wide by 8cm (3¼in) high

ABBREVIATIONS
See page 126.

cute accessories & gifts

MUSHROOM

CAP
Using A, make a magic ring.
Round 1: 6dc in magic ring. *(6 sts)*
Round 2: [2dc in next st] 6 times. *(12 sts)*
Round 3: [1dc, 2dc in next st] 6 times. *(18 sts)*
Round 4: [2dc, 2dc in next st] 6 times. *(24 sts)*
Round 5: [3dc, 2dc in next st] 6 times. *(30 sts)*
Rounds 6–11: 1dc in each st around.
Fasten off and sew in the ends (see page 120).

SMALL SPOTS
(make 4)
Using B, make a magic ring.
Round 1: 6dc in magic ring. *(6 sts)*
Fasten off leaving a long tail to sew to cap.

LARGE SPOTS
(make 2)
Using B, make a magic ring.
Round 1: 6dc in magic ring. *(6 sts)*
Round 2: [2dc in next st] 6 times. *(12 sts)*
Fasten off leaving a long tail to sew to cap.

HANGING LOOP
Using A, ch11.
Row 1: Slst in second ch from hook, 9slst. *(10 sts)*
Fasten off leaving a long tail to sew to top of cap.

HOUSE
Using C, ch13.
Round 1: 3dc in second ch from hook, 10dc, 3dc in last ch, working along opp side of chain, 10dc, slst in first dc. *(26 sts)*
Rounds 2–14: 1dc in each st around.
Fasten off leaving a long tail to sew to inside of cap.

DOOR
Using D, ch5.
Round 1: 1dc in second ch from hook, 2dc, 3dc in last ch, working along opp side of chain, 3dc.
Fasten off leaving a long tail to sew to house.

FINISHING
Sew spots onto cap. Thread a split ring onto loop, bring ends of loop together and sew to top of cap.
Using A, stitch a French knot (see page 126) for door handle.
Using E, stitch 2 simple windows above door, measuring 3 sts wide by 3 rows high.
Sew in all ends.

strawberry water bottle cover

Brighten up your day with this fun and colourful cover for your water bottle. The pattern features 3D stitches, a sewn-on strawberry motif and a simple crocheted drawstring cord to keep your bottle safe.

SKILL RATING ●●●

YARN AND MATERIALS
Knitcraft Cotton Blend DK (50% cotton, 50% acrylic) DK (light worsted) weight yarn, 215m (235yd) per 100g (3½oz) ball

1 ball in each of:
Yellow 1008 (A)
Hot Pink 1003 (B)
Teal 1002 (C)
Bright Blue 1005 (D)

Large wooden bead

HOOK AND EQUIPMENT
4mm (US size G/6) crochet hook
Yarn needle

FINISHED MEASUREMENTS
24cm (9½in) by 26cm (10¼in) circumference

ABBREVIATIONS
See page 126.

MAIN COVER
Using A, make a magic ring.
Round 1: 6dc into ring. *(6 dc)*
Round 2: [2dc in next st] 6 times. *(12 dc)*
Round 3: [1dc, 2dc in next st] 6 times. *(18 dc)*
Round 4: [2dc, 2dc in next st] 6 times. *(24 dc)*
Round 5: [3dc, 2dc in next st] 6 times. *(30 dc)*
Round 6: [4dc, 2dc in next st] 6 times. *(36 dc)*
Round 7: [5dc, 2dc in next st] 6 times. *(42 dc)*
Round 8: 1dcBLO in each st around.
Rounds 9-12: 1dc in each st around.
Line of strawberries
Join B and carry across round, do not fasten off A.
Round 13: [2dc in A, 5tr in B in next st] 14 times.
Fasten off B.
Join C and carry across round, do not fasten off A.
Round 14: [2dc in A, tr5tog in C] 14 times.
Fasten off C, cont in A.
Rounds 15-19: 1dc into each st around. *(42 dc)*
Fasten off A, join D.
Middle band
Rounds 20-31: Rep Round 15.
Fasten off D, join A.
Rounds 32-36: Rep Round 15.
Line of strawberries
Rounds 37 and 38: Rep Rounds 13 and 14.
Fasten off B and C, do not fasten off A.
Rounds 39-43: Rep Round 15.
Round 44: [3dc, ch2, miss 2 sts] 8 times, 2dc. *(42 sts)*
Round 45: [3dc, 2dc in 2-ch sp] 8 times, 2dc. *(42 dc)*
Round 46: 1dc in each st around.
Round 47: [1dc, 2dc in next st] 21 times. *(63 dc)*
Rounds 48 and 49: 1dc in each st around.
Fasten off and sew in ends (see page 120).

cute accessories & gifts

CORD
Using D, ch100.
Row 1: 1slst in second ch from hook, 1slst in each ch to end. *(99 slst)*
Fasten off and sew in ends.

STRAWBERRY
Using B, make a magic ring.
Round 1: Ch3 (counts as 1tr), 12tr in ring, slst in top of beg 3-ch to join. *(13 tr)*
Round 2: Slst, (1htr, 1tr) in next st, [3dtr in next st] twice, [3tr in next st] twice, (2tr, 1dtr) in next st, ch1, (1dtr, 2tr) in next st, [3tr in next st] twice, [3dtr in next st] twice, (1tr, 1htr) in next st, slst in first slst to join. *(34 sts, one 1-ch sp)*
Fasten off leaving a long tail to sew to cover.

STALK
Round 1: Using C, [ch4, 1dc in second ch from hook, 2dc] 3 times, slst in first st to join.
Fasten off leaving a long tail to sew to strawberry.

FINISHING
Sew the strawberry to the middle band using the photograph as a guide. Sew the stalk to the top of the strawberry.
Thread the cord through the eyelet holes around the top of the cover, bringing both ends out of one eyelet. Thread both ends through the wooden bead, then knot each end.

With a pouch that doubles up as a game board, this little noughts-and-crosses-style set is perfect for travel. For this two-player game, each person has five matching pieces and takes turns placing a piece in one of the squares. The first person to get three in a row horizontally, vertically or diagonally is the winner! You could also make the bag on its own and use it for storing cosmetics or travel essentials.

sunshine and snails game

SKILL RATING ●●○

YARN AND MATERIALS
Rico Ricorumi DK (100% cotton) DK (light worsted) weight yarn, 58m (64yd) per 25g (1oz) ball

1 ball in each of:
Rose 008 (A)
Red 028 (B)
Blue 032 (C)
Tangerine 026 (D)
Berry 015 (E)
Pistachio 047 (F)
Pastel Yellow 062 (G)

2 wooden beads, 25mm (1in)
Small piece of felt in each of two colours

HOOK AND EQUIPMENT
3.5mm (US size E/4) crochet hook
Yarn needle
Pencil
Fabric scissors

FINISHED MEASUREMENTS
Bag: 24cm (9½in) square
Snail: 7cm (3in) wide x 5cm (2in) high
Sunshine: 6.5cm (2¾in) diameter

ABBREVIATIONS
See page 126.

BAG
Do not carry yarns across. Use a separate ball of yarn for each section.
Using A, ch15, using B, ch15, using A, ch16.
Row 1 (RS): 1dc in second ch from hook using A, 14dc using A, 15dc using B, 15dc using A, turn. *(45 dc)*
Rows 2-14: Ch1, 15dc using A, 15dc using B, 15dc using A, turn.
Fasten off all yarns. Join again as needed.
Rows 15-28: Ch1, 15dc using B, 15dc using A, 15dc using B, turn.
Fasten off all yarns. Join again as needed.
Rows 29-42: Ch1, 15dc using A, 15dc using B, 15dc using A, turn.
Fasten off all yarns, join D.
Rows 43-84: Ch1, 1dc in each st, turn.
Fasten off D and sew in ends (see page 120).
Define squares by working surface crochet/chain stitch (see page 123) along edges using C.
Fold panel in half, join C to top corner. Work 1dc in each row end, through both pieces to join sides of bag together (see page 122).
Rep on other side.
Fasten off and sew in the ends.

Top edging
Join C to top RH side of bag.
Work in continuous rounds.
Rounds 1-4: 1dc in each st. *(90 dc)*
Round 5 (drawstring holes): [2dc, miss 2 sts, ch2] 22 times, 2dc.
Round 6: [2dc, 2dc in 2ch-sp] 22 times, 2dc. *(90 dc)*
Rounds 7-9: 1dc in each st. *(90 dc)*
Fasten off and sew in ends.

DRAWSTRING
Using D, ch120.
Row 1: 1slst in second ch from hook, 1slst in each ch. *(119 slst)*
Fasten off and sew in ends.

SNAIL
(make 5)
Using E, make a magic ring.
Round 1: 6dc in ring. *(6 dc)*
Round 2: [2dc in same st] 6 times. *(12 dc)*
Round 3: [1dc, 2dc in next st] 6 times. *(18 dc)*
Round 4: [2dc, 2dc in next st] 6 times. *(24 dc)*
Fasten off E, join F.
Row 5: 9dc, turn.
Row 6: Ch1, (does not count as st), 3dc in first st, 8dc, (4tr, 2htr) in next st of snail shell (Round 4), miss next st of Round 4, 1dc, turn. *(18 sts)*
Row 7: Ch3, slst in second ch, slst in next ch, slst in dc, ch3, slst in second ch, 1dc in first of the 4tr from prev row, 2htr in next tr, (1htr, 1dc) in next tr, slst in next tr, slst in each rem st to end.
Fasten off and sew in ends.

SUNSHINE
(make 5)
Using G, make a magic ring.
Round 1: 6dc in ring. *(6 dc)*
Round 2: [2dc in same st] 6 times. *(12 dc)*
Round 3: [1dc, 2dc in next st] 6 times. *(18 dc)*
Round 4: [2dc, 2dc in next st] 6 times. *(24 dc)*
Round 5: [3dc, 2dc in next st] 6 times. *(36 dc)*
Fasten off G, join D.
Round 6: (1dc, ch3, 1dc) in first st, slst in next st, *(1dc, ch3, 1dc) in next st, slst in next st; rep from * 16 times.
Fasten off and sew in ends.

FINISHING
Thread drawstring in and out through holes in Round 5 of bag. Thread a 25mm (1in) wooden bead onto each end of cord and tie a knot below to secure. Using a contrasting colour felt, draw around each motif and cut out. Use fabric glue to stick to back of each motif.

CHAPTER 3
Beautiful Wreaths & Decorations

bee and flower mobile

Add a playful touch to any room with this colourful and unique decoration. You could personalise your mobile by adding crocheted pieces from different projects, such as the heart from page 108 or mushrooms from page 110.

SKILL RATING ● ● ○

YARN AND MATERIALS
Rico Ricorumi DK (100% cotton) DK (light worsted) weight yarn, 58m (64yd) per 25g (1oz) ball

1 ball in each of:
White 001 (A)
Green 049 (B)
Yellow 006 (C)
Fuchsia 014 (D)
Sky Blue 031 (E)
Chocolate 057 (F)

15cm (6in) embroidery hoop
23cm (9in) embroidery hoop
11 natural wooden beads, 25mm (1in) diameter
Small amount of fibre filling
Fabric glue if required

HOOK AND EQUIPMENT
3mm (US size C/2-D/3) crochet hook
Yarn needle

FINISHED MEASUREMENTS
Bee: 10cm (4in) long
Daisy: 7.5cm (3in) diameter
Rainbow: 9cm (3½in) wide x 9cm (3½in) tall

ABBREVIATIONS
See page 126.

SPECIAL ABBREVIATION
Picot: Ch3, sl st in second ch from hook, sl st in next ch.

CLOUDS
Using A, ch81.
Round 1: 1dc in second ch from hook, 79dc to end. *(80 dc)*
Round 2: [Slst, miss 2 sts, 8dtr in next st, miss 2 sts, slst, miss 1 st, 6tr in next st, miss 1 st] 8 times.
Fasten off and sew in ends (see page 120).

VINE
Using B, ch94.
Round 1: Slst in second ch from hook, [4slst in main ch, ch6, slst in second ch from hook, 4slst] 23 times, working along opp side of foundation ch, [ch6, slst in second ch from hook, 4slst, 4slst in main ch] 23 times.
Fasten off and sew in ends.

BEE
BEE BODY
(make 1 each in C, D, E)
Using first colour, make a magic ring.
Round 1: 6dc in magic ring. *(6 dc)*
Round 2: [2dc in next st] 6 times. *(12 dc)*
Round 3: [1dc, 2dc in next st] 6 times. *(18 dc)*
Round 4: [2dc, 2dc in next st] 6 times. *(24 dc)*
Rounds 5-10: 1dc in each st.
Round 11: [2dc, dc2tog] 6 times. *(18 dc)*
Round 12: [1dc, dc2tog] 6 times. *(12 dc)*
Start to stuff with fibre filling.
Round 13: [Dc2tog] 6 times. *(6 dc)*
Change to F, do not fasten off first colour.
Round 14: Working in FLO, [2dc in next st] 6 times. *(12 dc)*
Round 15: [1dc, 2dc in next st] 6 times. *(18 dc)*
Round 16: [2dc, 2dc in next st] 6 times. *(24 dc)*
Change to first colour, do not fasten off F.

Rounds 17-19: 1dc in each st.
Change to F, do not fasten off first colour.
Rounds 20-22: 1dc in each st.
Change to first colour, fasten off F.
Round 23: [2dc, dc2tog] 6 times. *(18 dc)*
Round 24: [1dc, dc2tog] 6 times. *(12 dc)*
Continue to stuff with fibre filling.
Round 25: [Dc2tog] 6 times. *(6 dc)*
Fasten off, sew closed, sew in ends.

WING
(make 2 for each bee)
Using A, make a magic ring.
Round 1: 6dc in magic ring. *(6 dc)*
Round 2: [2dc in next st] 6 times. *(12 dc)*
Rounds 3-6: 1dc in each st.
Round 7: [2dc, dc2tog] 3 times. *(9 dc)*
Round 8: [1dc, dc2tog] 3 times. *(6 dc)*
Fasten off, sew closed, leaving long tail to sew to body of bee.

ANTENNAE
(make 1 for each bee)
Using F, ch12.
Fasten off.
Using needle, pull ch through top of bee's head to two equal lengths, forming two antennae.

DAISY
(make 6)
Using C, make a magic ring.
Round 1: 6dc in magic ring. *(6 dc)*
Round 2: [2dc in next st] 6 times. *(12 dc)*
Round 3: [1dc, 2dc in next st] 6 times. *(18 dc)*
Round 4: [2dc, 2dc in next st] 6 times. *(24 dc)*
Petals
Fasten off C, join A to any st.
Round 5: *(1dc, ch1, 1tr, 1dtr) in next dc, (1dtr, 1tr, ch1, 1dc) in next dc, 1dc; rep from * 7 more times.
Fasten off leaving long end for sewing flowers tog.

88 beautiful wreaths & decorations

LEAVES

(make 6)

Using B, ch9.

Round 1: 1dc in second ch from hook, 1htr, 2tr, 3dtr in next ch, 2tr, (2tr, picot, 2tr) in last ch, working along opp side of ch, 2tr, 3dtr in next ch, 2tr, 1htr, 1dc, slst in first dc, ch4, slst in second ch from hook, 2slst. Fasten off leaving long end for sewing leaves tog.

RAINBOW

(make 2)

Using E, ch16.

Row 1: 1dc in second ch from hook, 5dc, [2dc in next st] 3 times, 6dc, ch1, turn. *(18 dc)*

Row 2: 6dc, [1dc, 2dc in next st] 3 times, 6dc, ch1, turn. *(21 dc)*

Fasten off E, join B.

Row 3: 6dc, [2dc, 2dc in next st] 3 times, 6dc, ch1, turn. *(24 dc)*

Row 4: 6dc, [3dc, 2dc in next st] 3 times, 6dc, ch1, turn. *(27 dc)*

Fasten off B, join C.

Row 5: 6dc, [4dc, 2dc in next st] 3 times, 6dc, ch1, turn. *(30 dc)*

Row 6: 6dc, [5dc, 2dc in next st] 3 times, 6dc, ch1, turn. *(33 dc)*

Fasten off C, join D.

Row 7: 6dc, [6dc, 2dc in next st] 3 times, 6dc, ch1, turn. *(36 dc)*

Row 8: 6dc, [7dc, 2dc in next st] 3 times, 6dc, turn. *(39 dc)*

Fasten off leaving long end to sew rainbows tog.

FINISHING

Glue clouds around 15cm (9in) embroidery hoop.

Glue vine around 23cm (6in) embroidery hoop.

Sew or glue two flowers WS tog so you have three flowers in total.

Sew or glue two leaves WS tog so you have three leaves in total.

Sew two rainbows WS tog using D, so you have one rainbow.

Cut four 100cm (40in) lengths of A. Knot all four lengths tog at top with first bead.

Middle hanging length

Thread and glue one bead 8cm (3in) from first bead. Thread on rainbow, 20cm (8in) from second bead. Evenly space and glue three more beads below rainbow. Middle hanging length should measure 45cm (18in), cut excess off.

Three side lengths

Must be identical or mobile may not hang evenly. Thread and glue one bead 8cm (3in) from first bead on all three lengths. Leave gap of 8cm (3in) then attach cloud hoop. Leave another gap of 7cm (2¾in) before attaching leaves. Attach vines hoop 7cm (2¾in) below leaves. Leave 10cm (4in) and attach bees, another 10cm (4in) gap and glue final beads. Lastly attach flowers after another 10cm (4in) gap.

With its beautiful autumnal colours, this versatile decoration would look gorgeous hanging on a door or displayed on a mantelpiece. This pattern uses loop stitch to create the grass and is a great way of practising this technique.

mushroom wall décor

SKILL RATING ● ● ○

YARN AND MATERIALS
Rico Ricorumi DK (100% cotton) DK (light worsted) weight yarn, 58m (64yd) per 25g (1oz) ball

1 ball in each of:
Fox 025 (A)
White 001 (B)
Smokey Rose 010 (C)
Mustard 064 (D)
Pea 077 (E)
Sky Blue 031 (F)

25cm (10in) diameter embroidery hoop

HOOK AND EQUIPMENT
3mm (US size C/2-D/3) crochet hook
Yarn needle

FINISHED MEASUREMENTS
Small mushroom: 7cm (3in) tall
Medium mushroom: 10cm (4in) tall
Large mushroom: 12.5cm (45¾in) tall

ABBREVIATIONS
See page 126.

SPECIAL ABBREVIATION
Loop st (loop stitch): With the yarn over left index finger, insert the hook into the next st and draw two strands through the st (take the first strand from under the index finger and at the same time take the second strand from over the index finger). Pull the yarn to tighten loop, forming a 4-cm (1½-in) loop on index finger. Remove your finger from the loop, put the loop to the back of the work, yrh and pull through 3 loops on the hook (1 loop stitch made on right side of work).

SMALL MUSHROOM
CAP
Using A, make a magic ring.
Round 1: 6dc in magic ring. *(6 dc)*
Round 2: [2dc in next st] 6 times. *(12 dc)*
Round 3: 1dc in each st around.
Round 4: [1dc, 2dc in next st] 6 times. *(18 dc)*
Round 5: 1dc in each st around.
Round 6: [2dc, 2dc in next st] 6 times. *(24 dc)*
Round 7: 1dc in each st around.
Round 8: [3dc, 2dc in next st] 6 times. *(30 dc)*
Rounds 9 and 10: 1dc in each st around.
Fasten off and sew in ends (see page 120).

STALK
Using B, make a magic ring.
Round 1: 6dc in magic ring. *(6 dc)*
Round 2: [2dc in next st] 6 times. *(12 dc)*
Round 3: 1dcBLO in each st around
Rounds 4–15: 1dc in each st around.
Round 16: [Dc2tog] 6 times. *(6 dc)*
Fasten off and sew closed, leaving long tail to sew to cap.

90 beautiful wreaths & decorations

MEDIUM MUSHROOM
CAP
Using C, make a magic ring.
Rounds 1-8: Rep Rounds 1-8 of small mushroom. *(30 dc)*
Round 9: 1dc in each st around.
Round 10: [4dc, 2dc in next st] 6 times. *(36 dc)*
Rounds 11 and 12: 1dc in each st around.
Fasten off and sew in ends.

STALK
Using B, make a magic ring.
Round 1: 6dc in magic ring. *(6 dc)*
Round 2: [2dc in next st] 6 times. *(12 dc)*
Round 3: [1dc, 2dc in next st] 6 times. *(18 dc)*
Round 4: 1dcBLO in each st around.
Rounds 5-18: 1dc in each st around.
Round 19: [1dc, dc2tog] 6 times. *(12 dc)*
Round 20: [Dc2tog] 6 times. *(6 dc)*
Fasten off and sew closed, leaving long tail to sew to cap.

LARGE MUSHROOM
CAP
Using D, make a magic ring.
Rounds 1-8: Rep Rounds 1-8 of small mushroom. *(30 dc)*
Round 9: 1dc in each st around.
Round 10: [4dc, 2dc in next st] 6 times. *(36 dc)*
Round 11: 1dc in each st around.
Round 12: [5dc, 2dc in next st] 6 times. *(42 dc)*
Rounds 13 and 14: 1dc in each st around.
Fasten off and sew in ends.

STALK
Using B, make a magic ring.
Round 1: 6dc in magic ring. *(6 dc)*
Round 2: [2dc in next st] 6 times. *(12 dc)*
Round 3: [1dc, 2dc in next st] 6 times. *(18 dc)*
Round 4: [2dc, 2dc in next st] 6 times. *(24 dc)*
Round 5: 1dcBLO in each st around.
Rounds 6-21: 1dc in each st around.
Round 22: [2dc, dc2tog] 6 times. *(18 dc)*
Round 23: [1dc, dc2tog] 6 times. *(12 dc)*
Round 24: [Dc2tog] 6 times. *(6 dc)*

beautiful wreaths & decorations

Fasten off and sew closed, leaving long tail to sew to cap.

SMALL SPOTS
(make 4 in each of D, C, A)
Make a magic ring.
Round 1: 6dc in magic ring. *(6 dc)*
Fasten off.

BIG SPOTS
(make 1 in A, 2 in C)
Make a magic ring.
Round 1: 6dc in magic ring. *(6 dc)*
Round 2: [2dc in next st] 6 times. *(12 dc)*
Fasten off.

GRASS
Using E, ch41.
Row 1: 1dc in second ch from hook, 1dc in each ch to end, ch1, turn. *(40 dc)*
Row 2: Work loop st in each st, ch1, turn *(40 loop sts)*
Row 3: 1dc in each st, ch1, turn.
Rows 4-7: Rep Rows 2 and 3 twice more.
Row 8: Work loop st (see page 125) in each st.
Fasten off leaving long tail to sew around bottom of embroidery hoop.

BOW
Using F, ch61.
Row 1: Slst in second ch from hook, 59 slst. *(60 slst)*
Fasten off and sew in ends.

FINISHING
Sew grass around bottom part of embroidery hoop.
Sew 4 small spots in D to small cap, then sew cap to stalk.
Sew 4 small spots, 1 large spot in A to medium cap, then sew cap to stalk.
Sew 4 small spots, 2 large spots in C to large cap, then sew cap to stalk.
Sew mushrooms in size order along grass.
Tie bow around top of hoop.

mushroom wall décor

Decorate your home with beautiful spring flowers all year round with this pot of crocheted blooms. Yarn is wrapped around pieces of wire to create the stems, and crocheted soil is added to the pot. Several of these flowers tied together with ribbon would make a lovely birthday gift.

blooming lovely flower pot

SKILL RATING ● ● ●

YARN AND MATERIALS
Rico Ricorumi DK (100% cotton) DK (light worsted) weight yarn, 58m (64yd) per 25g (1oz) ball

1 ball in each of:
Orchid 016 (A)
Pastel Yellow 062 (B)
White 001 (C)
Green 049 (D)
Candy Pink 012 (E)
Red 028 (F)
Berry 015 (G)
Pistachio 047 (H)
Pea 077 (I)
Chocolate 057 (J)

8 lengths of wire, each 35cm (13¾in) long

Fibre filling

Terracotta plant pot

HOOK AND EQUIPMENT
3.5mm (US size E/4) crochet hook

Yarn needle

Glue gun

FINISHED MEASUREMENTS
Lavender: 33cm (13in)
Daisy: 27cm (10½in)
Tulip: 29cm (11½in)
Leafy sprig: 34cm (13½in)

ABBREVIATIONS
See page 126.

LAVENDER
(make 2)
Using A, ch100.
Starting in second ch from hook, (slst, 3ch, slst) in each st to end.
Fasten off and sew in ends (see page 120).

DAISY
(make 2)
Using B, make a magic ring.
Round 1: 6dc in magic ring. *(6 dc)*
Round 2: [2dc in next st] 6 times. *(12 dc)*
Round 3: [1dc, 2dc in next st] 6 times. *(18 dc)*
Round 4: [2dc, 2dc in next st] 6 times. *(24 dc)*
Petals
Fasten off B, join C.
Round 5: *slst, (slst, ch3, 1dtr) in next st, (1dtr, ch3, slst) in next st; rep from * 7 more times.
Fasten off and sew in ends.

DAISY LEAF
(make 4)
Using D, ch6.
Row 1: 1dc in second ch from hook, 1htr, 2tr in next ch, 1tr, 4tr in last ch, working along opp side of chain, 1tr, 2tr in next ch, 1htr, 1dc, slst in first dc.
Fasten off leaving a long tail to attach to stem.

TULIP
(make 1 in each of E, F, G)
Make a magic ring.
Round 1: 6dc in magic ring. *(6 dc)*
Round 2: [2dc in next st] 6 times. *(12 dc)*
Round 3: [1dc, 2dc in next st] 6 times. *(18 dc)*
Round 4: [2dc, 2dc in next st] 6 times. *(24 dc)*
Rounds 5-16: 1dc in each st.
Fasten off leaving a long tail to sew closed.

TULIP LEAF
(make 3)
Using H, ch24.
Round 1: 1dc in second ch from hook, 1htr, 20tr, 4tr in last ch, working along opp side of chain, 20tr, 1htr, 1dc.
Fasten off and sew in ends.

LEAFY SPRIG
(make 13)
Using I, ch6.
Row 1: 1dc in the second ch from hook, 1htr, 1tr, 1htr, (1dc, slst) in last ch.
Fasten off leaving a long tail to attach to stem.

SOIL
Using J, ch6, join with slst to make a ring.
Round 1: 12dc in ring (this creates centre hole for flower stems). *(12 sts)*
Round 2: [1dc, 2dc in next st] 6 times. *(18 sts)*
Round 3: [2dc, 2dc in next st] 6 times. *(24 sts)*
Round 4: [3dc, 2dc in next st] 6 times. *(30 sts)*
Round 5: [4dc, 2dc in next st] 6 times. *(36 sts)*
Round 6: [5dc, 2dc in next st] 6 times. *(42 sts)*
Round 7: [6dc, 2dc in next st] 6 times. *(48 sts)*
Round 8: [7dc, 2dc in next st] 6 times. *(54 sts)*

Round 9: [8dc, 2dc in next st] 6 times. *(60 sts)*
Round 10: 1dc in each st around.

FINISHING

Using a glue gun, wrap each lavender strip around a length of wire, gluing as you go. It should cover about one third of length. Using D, wrap around rest of wire, gluing in place as you go.

Fasten each daisy head to top of a wire and glue in place. Wrap wire with D, wrapping along whole length of and adding two leaves to each stem, hiding yarn ends as you go.

Insert a length of wire in each tulip head, bend over top of wire and glue in place inside tulip head. Lightly stuff with fibre filling. Press two sides of the top together and sew in place. Now press other two sides together and sew in place, to form a cross shape for top of tulip. Using H, wrap around the rest of the length of wire below the tulip heads, adding one leaf and gluing in place as you go.

Add leafy sprigs around top third of remaining wire and cont to wrap using I down stem.

Use some fibre filling to stuff terracotta pot.

Thread all finished flowers through centre hole in soil and glue stem ends before pushing inside pot. Glue soil to inside rim of pot.

SKILL RATING ● ○ ○

YARN AND MATERIALS
Rico Ricorumi DK (100% cotton) DK (light worsted) weight yarn, 58m (64yd) per 25g (1oz) ball

1 ball in each of:
Fuchsia 014 (A)
Yellow 006 (B)
Sky Blue 031 (C)

30cm (12in) diameter circular mirror

HOOK AND EQUIPMENT
3.5mm (US size E/4) crochet hook

Yarn needle

Glue gun

FINISHED MEASUREMENTS
Each flower: 5.5cm (2¼in) across

ABBREVIATIONS
See page 126.

COLOURWAYS
Fuchsia with Yellow centre
Sky Blue with Fuchsia centre
Yellow with Sky Blue centre

daisy chain mirror

Add a splash of colour to a plain mirror with this simple design. The flowers are quick to make, and you can get creative by mixing and matching your colours for each one. The finished design would make a beautiful centrepiece for any room.

FLOWERS
(make 4 of each colourway)
Using centre colour, make a magic ring.
Round 1: Ch3 (counts as first tr), 1tr, ch1, *2tr, ch1; rep from * 4 more times.
Fasten off centre colour, join petal colour in ch sp from Round 1 and work in each ch sp around.
Round 2: [Slst into ch sp, ch3] 6 times, slst into first slst to join.
Round 3: Working in 3 ch sps from Round 2, [slst, ch2, 3tr, ch2, slst] in each ch-sp to create 6 petals.
Fasten off and sew in ends (see page 120).

FINISHING
Glue all flowers around mirror using glue gun.

Bring the outdoors inside with this pretty garland embellished with 3D roses. Hooked up in beautiful chunky yarn, this garland would look lovely strung from the ceiling, hung on a door or draped across a table.

roses garland

SKILL RATING ● ● ○

YARN AND MATERIALS
Knitcraft Return Of Mac Yarn (100% cotton) chunky (bulky) weight yarn, 81m (88½yd) per 200g (7oz) ball

    1 ball of Sage 1007 (A)

Knitcraft Join the Dots (80% acrylic, 20% wool) chunky (bulky) weight yarn, 190m (208yd) per 100g (3½oz) ball

    1 ball in each of:
    Cream Print 1002 (B)
    Purple Print 1000 (C)
    Blue Print 1003 (D)

HOOK AND EQUIPMENT
6mm (US size J/10) crochet hook
Yarn needle

FINISHED MEASUREMENTS
Flower: 9cm (3½in) across
Leaf: 11cm (4¼in) long
Garland: 120cm (47¼in) long

ABBREVIATIONS
See page 126.

SPECIAL ABBREVIATION
Picot: Ch3, slst in second ch from hook, slst in next ch.

GARLAND
Using A, ch122.
Row 1: 1htr in third ch from hook, 1htr in each ch to end. *(120 htr)*
Fasten off and sew in ends (see page 120).

LEAVES
(make 14)
Using B, ch9.
Round 1: 1tr in fifth ch from hook (missed 4 ch counts as 1 tr and one foundation ch), 3tr, (2tr 1dtr, picot, 1dtr, 2tr) in last ch, working along opp side of chain, 4tr, 4tr in beg foundation ch, sl st to in third ch of beg tr to join.
Fasten off and sew in ends.

ROSE
(make 4 in C, 3 in D)
Ch25.
Row 1: 1tr in fifth ch from hook (missed 4 ch counts as 1tr, ch2), *miss next ch, (1tr, ch2, 1tr) in next ch; rep from * 9 times, turn. *(11 v-sts)*
Row 2: Ch1, 6tr in first 2-ch sp, *1dc between next 2 tr, 6tr in next 2-ch sp; rep from * to end. *(11 petals)*
Fasten off leaving a long tail.

FINISHING
Roll rose from one end and stitch in place.
Using photo as a guide, sew pair of leaves and alternate colour rose spaced at intervals along garland.
Sew in ends.

Go bright and colourful with this fantastic floral bunting. The pattern uses granny stitches to create the triangle shapes, and the pieces are crocheted together along the top so no sewing up is required!

daisy chain bunting

BUNTING TRIANGLES
(make 6)
Using A, make a magic ring.
Round 1: Ch3 (counts as 1tr), 11tr in ring. *(12 tr (6 x 2-tr sets))*
Fasten off A, join B between 2-tr sets from Round 1.
Round 2: [1dc between 2-tr sets, ch3] 6 times, slst in first dc to join.
Round 3: Working in 3-ch sps from Round 2, *(slst, ch3, 3dtr, ch3, slst) in 3-ch sp, ch1; rep from * 5 times, slst around first 3-ch to join. *(6 petals)*
Fasten off B, join C in 1-ch sp from Round 3.
Round 4: (Slst, ch3) in each 1-ch sp from Round 3, slst around first ch-3 to join.

SKILL RATING ● ● ○

YARN AND MATERIALS
Women's Institute Premium Acrylic Yarn (100% acrylic) DK (light worsted) weight yarn, 250m (273yd) per 100g (3½oz) ball

1 ball in each of:
Yellow 1025 (A)
White 1000 (B)
Green 1001 (C)
Soft Pink 1026 (D)
Soft Blue 1025 (E)

HOOK AND EQUIPMENT
4mm (US size G/6) crochet hook
Yarn needle

FINISHED MEASUREMENTS
Triangle: 18cm (7in) wide by 16cm (6¼in) tall
Bunting: 186cm (73in) long

ABBREVIATIONS
See page 126.

102   beautiful wreaths & decorations

Round 5: (Ch4 (counts as 1dtr), 2dtr, ch2, 3dtr) in first 3-ch sp (corner), ch2, 3htr in next 3-ch sp, *(3dtr, ch2, 3dtr) in next 3-ch sp, ch2, 3htr in next 3-ch sp; rep from * once more, slst in fourth ch of beg ch-4 to join.

Round 6: Ch4 (counts as 1tr, ch1), *(3tr, ch2, 3tr) in first 2-ch sp (corner), ch1, 3tr in next 2-ch sp, ch1, 3tr in next 2-ch sp, ch1; rep from * once more, (3tr, ch2, 3tr) in next 2-ch sp, ch1, 3tr in next 2-ch sp, ch1, 2tr in next 2-ch sp, slst in third ch of beg 4-ch to join.
Fasten off C, join D in any 2-ch corner sp.

Round 7: Ch2 (counts as first htr in foll instructions), work (3htr, ch2, 3htr) in each corner sp, 1htr in top of each tr from Round 6 and 1tr in each 1-ch sp, all around, slst in first st to join. *(63 sts, three 2-ch sp)*

Round 8: Ch1 (does not count as a st), 1dc in each st around and (2dc, ch1, 2dc) in each corner sp to end, slst in first st to join. *(75 sts, three 1-ch sp)*
Fasten off D, join E in any corner 1-ch sp.

Round 9: Ch 1 (does not count as a st), 1dc in 1-ch sp, miss next st, *(ch3, 1dc) in next st, miss next st/sp; rep from * along two sides of triangle, ending with 1dc in last 1-ch sp.

Fasten off and sew in ends (see page 120).

FINISHING
Using E, ch40.
Row 1: *1dc in each dc in top (last side) of triangle, ch5; rep from * to join each triangle, ch40, turn.
Row 2: Starting in second ch, 1dc in each ch and st to end, ch1, turn.
Row 3: *1dc, ch3, miss next st; rep from * to end, ending with 1dc in last st.
Fasten off and sew in the ends.

SKILL RATING ● ○ ○

YARN AND MATERIALS
Rico Ricorumi DK (100% cotton) DK (light worsted) weight yarn, 58m (64yd) per 25g (1oz) ball
   1 ball in each of:
   Red 028 (A)
   Yellow 006 (B)
   Green 049 (C)
   Sky Blue 031 (D)
   Orchid 016 (E)
   Candy Pink 012 (F)
   Lilac 017 (G)

HOOK AND EQUIPMENT
3.5mm (US size E/4) crochet hook
Yarn needle

FINISHED MEASUREMENTS
Approx 76cm (30in) long

ABBREVIATIONS
See page 126.

Update your décor with this quick and simple paper-chain-style decoration. This is a great stashbuster project, and you could add a new link whenever you have spare yarn to use up. Crochet one of these in Christmas shades to make a festive version that you can bring out every year.

frilly crochet chain

CHAIN LINK
(make 3 in each of colours A, B, C, D, E and F)
For each chain link, crochet through prev chain link to attach tog. Make all links in same way, changing colours for each.
Ch20, slst in first ch to form a ring.
Rounds 1-3: Ch1 (does not count as st), 1htr in each st around, slst in first st to join. *(20 htr)*
Fasten off.
Frill first side
Join G to any st.
Round 4: [1dc, miss 1 st, ch3] to end of round.
Fasten off.
Frill second side
Rep frill first side on other side of chain link.

FINISHING
Sew in ends (see page 120).

With sweet ladybirds, daisies and a mini heart, this adorable multicoloured wreath would look wonderful hung up on a door or displayed on a shelf. You could even use the rainbow wreath as a base and decorate it with different embellishments such as the forget-me-nots and roses from pages 112–113.

rainbow wreath

SKILL RATING ● ● ●

YARN AND MATERIALS
Rico Ricorumi DK (100% cotton) DK (light worsted) weight yarn, 58m (64yd) per 25g (1oz) ball
1 ball in each of:
  Purple 020 (A)
  Lilac 017 (B)
  Pink 011 (C)
  Red 028 (D)
  Smokey Orange 024 (E)
  Tangerine 026 (F)
  Yellow 006 (G)
  Pastel Green 045 (H)
  Turquoise 039 (I)
  Light Blue 033 (J)
  White 001 (K)
  Grass Green 044 (L)
  Black 060 (M)
  Sky Blue 031 (N)

30cm (12in) polystyrene wreath base

2 pairs of safety eyes, 8mm (½in) diameter

Fibre filling

HOOK AND EQUIPMENT
3.5mm (US size E/4) crochet hook
Yarn needle

FINISHED MEASUREMENTS
30cm (12in) diameter

ABBREVIATIONS
See page 126.

WREATH COVER
Work in a random rainbow colour order using yarns A–J, varying number of rows in each colour.
Ch36.
Row 1: 1dc in second ch from hook, 34dc, turn. *(35 dc)*
Rows 2–184: Ch1 (does not count as st throughout), 1dc in each st to end, turn.
Row 185: Ch1, 1dc in each st to end.
Fasten off leaving long tail to sew Row 1 to Row 185.

LARGE DAISY
(make 4)
Using G, make a magic ring.
Round 1: 6dc in ring. *(6 dc)*
Round 2: 2dc in each st. *(12 dc)*
Round 3: [1dc, 2dc in next st] 6 times. *(18 dc)*
Fasten off G, join K.
Round 4: *(Slst, ch4, 2dtr) in first st, (2dtr, ch4, slst) in next st, slst; rep from * 5 times.
Fasten off.

LARGE LEAVES
(make 4)
Using L, ch10.
Round 1: 1dc in second ch, 1dc, 1htr, 1tr, 1dtr, 1tr, 1htr, 1dc, 3dc in last ch, working along opp side of chain, 1dc, 1htr, 1tr, 1dtr, 1tr, 1htr, 1dc, 2dc in last ch, slst in first dc.
Round 2: Ch1, 1dc in same st, 1dc, 1htr, 2tr in next st, 3tr in next st, 2tr in next st, 3htr, (2htr, ch2, 2htr) in next st, 3htr, 2tr in next st, 3tr in next st, 2tr in next st, 1htr, 2dc, 3dc in next st, slst in first st.
Fasten off and sew in ends (see page 120).

106 beautiful wreaths & decorations

rainbow wreath 107

SMALL DAISY
(make 3)
Using G, make a magic ring.
Round 1: 6dc in ring. *(6 dc)*
Round 2: 2dc in each st. *(12 dc)*
Fasten off G, join K.
Round 3: *(slst, ch3, 2tr, ch3, slst) in first st, slst; rep from * 5 times.
Fasten off.

SMALL LEAVES
(make 7)
Using L, ch9.
Round 1: 1dc in second ch from hook, 1htr, 1tr, 2dtr, 1tr, 1htr, 3dc in last ch, working along opp side of chain, 1htr, 1tr, 2dtr, 1tr, 1htr, 1dc, slst in first st.
Fasten off and sew in ends.

HEART
Using D, make a magic ring.
Round 1: Ch3 (counts as a tr), 3dtr, 3tr, ch1, 1dtr, ch1, 3tr, 3dtr, ch3, slst in ring.
Fasten off and sew in ends.

LADYBIRD
HEAD AND BODY
(make 2)
Using M, make a magic ring.
Round 1: 6dc in ring. *(6 dc)*
Round 2: 2dc in each st. *(12 dc)*
Round 3: [1dc, 2dc in next st] 6 times. *(18 dc)*
Round 4: [2dc, 2dc in next st] 6 times. *(24 dc)*
Round 5: [3dc, 2dc in next st] 6 times. *(30 dc)*
Rounds 6-11: 1dc in each st.
Insert safety eyes between Rounds 8 and 9, 6 sts apart.
Sew a simple mouth between Rounds 9 and 10, 3 sts apart.
Round 12: [3dc, dc2tog] 6 times. *(24 dc)*
Start to stuff with fibre filling.
Round 13: [2dc, dc2tog] 6 times. *(18 dc)*
Round 14: [1dc, dc2tog] 6 times. *(12 dc)*
Round 15: [Dc2tog] 6 times. *(6 dc)*
Round 16: 2dc in each st. *(12 dc)*
Round 17: [1dc, 2dc in next st] 6 times. *(18 dc)*
Round 18: [2dc, 2dc in next st] 6 times. *(24 dc)*
Rounds 19-24: 1dc in each st.
Round 25: [2dc, dc2tog] 6 times. *(18 dc)*
Round 26: [1dc, dc2tog] 6 times. *(12 dc)*
Round 27: [Dc2tog] 6 times. *(6 dc)*
Fasten off and sew gap closed.

WING
(make 4)
Using D, make a magic ring.
Round 1: 6dc in ring. *(6 dc)*
Round 2: 2dc in each st. *(12 dc)*
Round 3: [1dc, 2dc in next st] 6 times. *(18 dc)*
Rounds 4-6: 1dc in each st.
Round 7: [1dc, dc2tog] 6 times. *(12 dc)*
Rounds 8-10: 1dc in each st.
Round 11: [2dc, dc2tog] 3 times. *(9 dc)*
Rounds 12-13: 1dc in each st.
Fasten off leaving a tail to sew to body.

SPOT
(make 3 for each wing)
Using M, make a magic ring.
Round 1: 6dc in ring, slst in first st. *(6 dc)*
Fasten off leaving a tail to sew to wing.

ANTENNA
(make 2)
Using M, ch20
Row 1: Slst in second ch, 18 slst.
Fasten off leaving a tail to sew to head.

LEG
(make 4)
Using M, make a magic ring.
Round 1: 6dc in ring. *(6 dc)*
Round 2: 2dc in each st. *(12 dc)*
Rounds 3-4: 1dc in each st.
Round 5: [2dc, dc2tog] 3 times. *(9 dc)*
Round 6: [1dc, dc2tog] 3 times. *(6 dc)*
Rounds 7-10: 1dc in each st.
Lightly stuff with fibre filling.
Fasten off leaving a tail to sew to body.

ARM
(make 4)
Using M, make a magic ring.
Round 1: 6dc in ring. *(6 dc)*
Round 2: [1dc, 2dc in next st] 3 times. *(9 dc)*
Round 3: 1dc in each st.
Round 4: [1dc, dc2tog] 3 times. *(6 dc)*
Rounds 5-8: 1dc in each st.
Lightly stuff with fibre filling.
Fasten off leaving a tail to sew to body.

BOW TIE
(make 1)
Using N, make a magic ring.
Round 1: [Ch3, 3dtr, ch3, slst] twice in ring.
Fasten off leaving a long tail.

FINISHING
Sew short ends of wreath cover together to make ring. Place wreath cover around polystyrene wreath. Sew sides together to encase wreath. Sew in ends.
Using photo as a guide, sew daisies and leaves around bottom half of wreath.
Sew spots to wings, arms to each side of body, legs to underside of body and wings to back of each ladybird. Thread an antenna through top of each ladybird head and sew in place. Wrap tail of bowtie around middle four to six times, sew to secure and sew onto ladybird. Position both ladybirds on wreath and sew in place. Attach heart to top centre front of wreath.

gnome's washing wreath

Welcome guests to your home with this cute and quirky design. Gorgeous flowers, mini toadstools and a sun decorate the wreath and the mini gnome and washing line add adorable finishing touches.

SKILL RATING ● ● ●

YARN AND MATERIALS
Rico Ricorumi DK (100% cotton) DK (light worsted) weight yarn, 58m (64yd) per 25g (1oz) ball

1 ball in each of:
Wine Red 029 (A)
Beige 055 (B)
Blue 032 (C)
Silver Grey 058 (D)
Black 060 (E)
White 001 (F)
Yellow 006 (G)
Lilac 017 (H)
Orange 027 (I)
Smokey Orange 024 (J)
Tangerine 026 (K)
Fuchsia 014 (L)
Pink 011 (M)
Green 049 (N)
Pistachio 047 (O)
Caramel 053 (P)

Pair of safety eyes 10mm (½in) diameter
Fibre filling
String for washing line
6 miniature wooden pegs
Wicker wreath, 30cm (12in) diameter

HOOK AND EQUIPMENT
3.5mm (US size E/4) crochet hook
Yarn needle

FINISHED MEASUREMENTS
Wreath: 30cm (12in) diameter

ABBREVIATIONS
See page 126.

SPECIAL ABBREVIATION
PC (popcorn): work 6tr all in one st, remove live loop from hook, insert hook in top of first tr, place loop on hook and pull through.

GNOME
HAT
Using A, make a magic ring.
Round 1: 6dc in ring. *(6 dc)*
Round 2: 1dc in each st.
Round 3: [1dc, 2dc in next st] 3 times. *(9 dc)*
Round 4: 1dc in each st.
Round 5: [2dc, 2dc in next st] 3 times. *(12 dc)*
Round 6: 1dc in each st.
Round 7: [3dc, 2dc in next st] 3 times. *(15 dc)*
Round 8: 1dc in each st.
Round 9: [4dc, 2dc in next st] 3 times. *(18 dc)*
Fasten off leaving long tail to sew to head.

HEAD AND BODY
Using B, make a magic ring. Work in a continuous spiral.
Round 1: 6dc in ring. *(6 dc)*
Round 2: 2dc in each st. *(12 dc)*
Round 3: [1dc, 2dc in next st] 6 times. *(18 dc)*
Round 4: 1dc in each st.
Round 5: 9dc, PC, 8dc. *(18 sts)*
Round 6: Rep Round 4.
Insert safety eyes either side of nose.
Start to stuff with fibre filling.
Round 7: [1dc, dc2tog] 6 times. *(12 dc)*
Round 8: [Dc2tog] 6 times *(6 dc)*
Fasten off B, join C.
Round 9: 2dc in each st. *(12 dc)*
Round 10: [1dc, 2dc in next st] 6 times. *(18 dc)*
Rounds 11-13: 1dc in each st. *(18 dc)*
Fasten off C, join D.
Rounds 14 and 15: 1dc in each st.
Round 16: [1dc, dc2tog] 6 times. *(12 dc)*
Round 17: [Dc2tog] 6 times. *(6 dc)*
Fasten off and sew gap closed.

ARMS/LEGS
(make 2 in B/C for arms, 2 in E/D for legs)
Using B or E, make a magic ring.
Round 1: 6dc in ring. *(6 dc)*
Round 2: 1dc in each st.
Fasten off B or E, join C or D.
Rounds 3-8: 1dc in each st.
Do not stuff, fasten off leaving long tail to sew to body.

BEARD
Using F, make a magic ring.
Row 1: 3dc in ring, ch1, turn. *(3 dc)*
Row 2: 2dc in each st, ch1, turn. *(6 dc)*
Row 3: [1dc, 2dc in next st] 3 times. *(9 dc)*
Fasten off leaving long tail to sew beard to face.

GNOME'S WASHING
TROUSERS
Using P, make a magic ring.
Round 1: 6dc in ring. *(6 dc)*
Rounds 2-6: 1dc in each st.
Fasten off first leg.
Using P, make a magic ring.
Rep Rounds 1 to 6 for second leg, do not fasten off.
Cont working around first leg to join with second leg.
Rounds 7-10: 1dc in each st. *(12 dc)*
Fasten off and sew in ends (see page 120).

gnome's washing wreath

HAT
Using G, make a magic ring.
Round 1: 6dc in ring. *(6 dc)*
Round 2: 1dc in each st.
Round 3: [1dc, 2dc in next st] 3 times. *(9 dc)*
Round 4: 1dc in each st.
Round 5: [2dc, 2dc in next st] 3 times. *(12 dc)*
Round 6: 1dc in each st.
Round 7: [3dc, 2dc in next st] 3 times. *(15 dc)*
Rounds 8 and 9: 1dc in each st.
Fasten off and sew in ends.

JUMPER
Using A, ch10, slst in first ch to form a ring. *(10 sts)*
Round 1: Ch1 (does not count as a st throughout), *1dc, (1dc, ch1, 1dc), 2dc, (1dc, ch1, 1dc); rep from * once more, slst in first st. *(14 dc, 4 ch sps)*
Round 2: Ch1, 2dc, (1dc, ch1, 1dc) in ch sp, 4dc, (1dc, ch1, 1dc) in ch sp, 3dc, (1dc, ch1, 1dc) in ch sp, 4dc, (1dc, ch1, 1dc), 1dc, slst in first st. *(22 dc, 4 ch sps)*
Round 3: Ch1, 3dc, fold next two ch sps tog, insert hook through next 2 ch sps and work slst (missed sts will form sleeve), 5dc to next ch sp, insert hook through next 2 ch sps and work slst, 1dc in last 2 sts, slst in first st. *(10 dc)*
Round 4: Ch1, 2dc, [2dc in next st] twice, 3dc, [2dc in next st] twice, 1dc, slst in first st. *(14 dc)*
Rounds 5–7: Ch1, 14dc around, slst in first st.
Fasten off and sew in ends.
Sleeve
Join yarn to the underarm st of one set of missed sts from Round 3.
Round 1: Ch1, dc2tog, 2dc, dc2tog, slst in first st. *(4 dc)*
Rounds 2 and 3: Ch1, 4dc, slst in first st.
Fasten off.
Rep for second sleeve on other side.

FORGET-ME-NOT
(make 5 in C, 3 in H)
Using G, make a magic ring.
Round 1: Ch1 (does not count as st), 5dc in ring, slst in first dc. *(5 dc)*
Fasten off G, join C or H.
Round 2: (Ch2, 2tr, ch2, slst) in each st, slst in first st. *(5 petals)*
Fasten off and sew in ends.

LARGE MUSHROOM
CAP
Using I, make a magic ring.
Round 1: 6dc in ring. *(6 dc)*
Round 2: 2dc in each st. *(12 dc)*
Round 3: [1dc, 2dc in next st] 6 times. *(18 dc)*
Round 4: [2dc, 2dc in next st] 6 times. *(24 dc)*
Round 5: [3dc, 2dc in next st] 6 times *(30 dc)*
Rounds 6 and 7: 1dc in each st.
Fasten off and sew in ends.

STALK
Using F, make a magic ring.
Round 1: 6dc in ring. *(6 dc)*
Round 2: 2dc in each st. *(12 dc)*
Round 3: [1dc, 2dc in next st] 6 times. *(18 dc)*
Round 4: [2dcBLO, 2dcBLO in next st] 6 times. *(24 dc)*
Rounds 5–12: 1dc in each st.
Fasten off leaving long tail to sew to inside of cap, sew in ends.

MEDIUM MUSHROOM
CAP
Using J, make a magic ring.
Round 1: 6dc in ring. *(6 dc)*
Round 2: 2dc in each st. *(12 dc)*
Round 3: [1dc, 2dc in next st] 6 times. *(18 dc)*
Round 4: [2dc, 2dc in next st] 6 times. *(24 dc)*
Rounds 5 and 6: 1dc in each st.
Fasten off and sew in ends.

STALK
Using F, make a magic ring.
Round 1: 6dc in ring. *(6 dc)*
Round 2: 2dc in each st. *(12 dc)*
Round 3: [1dcBLO, 2dcBLO in next st] 6 times. *(18 dc)*
Rounds 4–9: 1dc in each st.
Fasten off leaving long tail to sew to inside of cap, sew in ends.

SMALL MUSHROOM
CAP
Using K, make a magic ring.
Round 1: 6dc in ring. *(6 dc)*
Round 2: 2dc in each st. *(12 dc)*
Round 3: [1dc, 2dc in next st] 6 times. *(18 dc)*
Rounds 4 and 5: 1dc in each st.
Fasten off and sew in ends.

STALK
Using F, make a magic ring.
Round 1: 6dc in ring. *(6 dc)*
Round 2: 2dcBLO in each st. *(12 dc)*

Rounds 3-6: 1dc in each st.
Fasten off leaving long tail to sew to inside of cap, sew in ends.

ROSES
FLOWER
(make 3 in L, 2 in M)
Ch25.
Row 1: 1tr in 5th ch from hook (counts as 1tr, ch2), *miss next ch, (1tr, ch2, 1tr) in next ch; rep from * 9 times, turn. *(11 v-sts)*
Row 2: Ch1, 6tr in first 2ch sp, *1dc between next 2 tr, 6tr in next 2-ch sp; rep from * to end. *(11 petals)*
Fasten off leaving a long tail.

LEAVES
(make 8 in N, 11 in O)
Ch9.
Round 1: 1dc in second ch from hook, 1htr, 1tr, 2dtr, 1tr, 1htr, 3dc in last ch, working along other side of chain, 1htr, 1tr, 2dtr, 1tr, 1htr, 1dc, slst in beg ch.
Fasten off and sew in ends.

SUNSHINE
(make 2)
Using K, make a magic ring.
Round 1: 6dc in ring. *(6 dc)*
Round 2: 2dc in each st. *(12 dc)*
Round 3: [1dc, 2dc in next st] 6 times. *(18 dc)*
Round 4: [2dc, 2dc in next st] 6 times. *(24 dc)*
Round 5: [3dc, 2dc in next st] 6 times *(30 dc)*
Round 6: [4dc, 2dc in next st] 6 times *(36 dc)*
Fasten off K, join J.
With both pieces WS tog, work Round 7 through both layers to join.
Stuff with fibre filling before closing.
Round 7: *Slst, [1dc, ch3, 1dc] in next st, rep from * 17 times, slst in first st.
Fasten off and sew in ends.

FINISHING
Sew hat on gnome's head and beard below nose.
Sew arms and legs to body.
Roll each rose from one end and stitch in place.
Using photo as a guide, stitch gnome, sunshine, leaves, roses and mushrooms in place.
Tie twine across wreath to make washing line.
Peg washing to line.

techniques

This section guides you through all the crochet and finishing techniques that you will need to make the projects in this book. If you're new to crochet, practise the skills covered in this section before you start on a project. Keep the loops of your stitches loose – you can work on creating an even tension (see page 117) across the fabric as you practise and develop your skills. Crochet has only a few basic stitches to master, and it is easy to undo if you go wrong because you only have one loop on the hook.

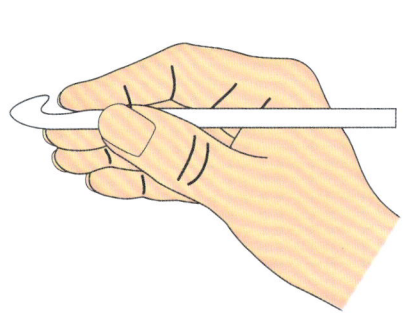
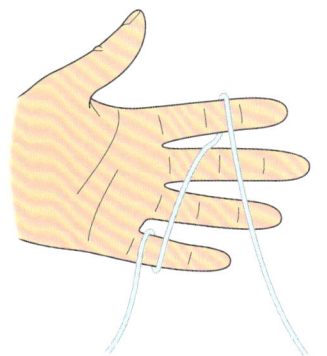
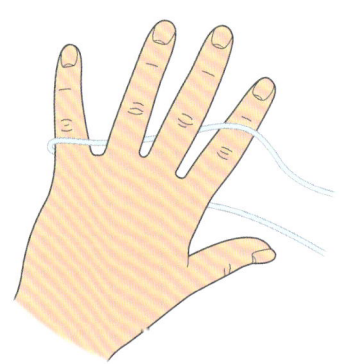

Holding the hook
Pick up your hook as though you are picking up a pen or pencil. Keeping the hook held loosely between your fingers and thumb, turn your hand so that the palm is facing up and the hook is balanced in your hand and resting in the space between your index finger and your thumb.

You can also hold the hook like a knife – this may be easier if you are working with a large hook or with chunky yarn. Choose the method that you find most comfortable.

Holding the yarn
1 Pick up the yarn with your little finger in the opposite hand to your hook, with your palm facing upward and with the short end in front. Turn your hand to face downward, with the yarn on top of your index finger and under the other two fingers and wrapped right around the little finger, as shown above.

2 Turn your hand to face you, ready to hold the work in your middle finger and thumb. Keeping your index finger only at a slight curve, hold the work or the slip knot using the same hand, between your middle finger and your thumb and just below the crochet hook and loop/s on the hook.

Holding the hook and yarn while crocheting
Keep your index finger, with the yarn draped over it, at a slight curve, and hold your work (or the slip knot) using the same hand, between your middle finger and your thumb and just below the crochet hook and loop/s on the hook.

As you draw the loop through the hook release the yarn on the index finger to allow the loop to stay loose on the hook. If you tense your index finger, the yarn will become too tight and pull the loop on the hook too tight for you to draw the yarn through.

Holding the hook and yarn for left-handers
Some left-handers learn to crochet like right-handers, but others learn with everything reversed – with the hook in the left hand and the yarn in the right.

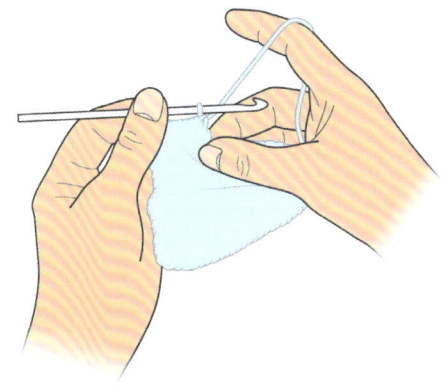

Making a slip knot

The simplest way is to make a circle with the yarn, so that the loop is facing downward.

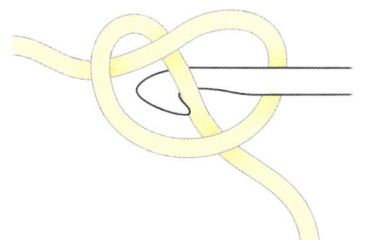

1 In one hand hold the circle at the top where the yarn crosses, and let the tail drop down at the back so that it falls across the centre of the loop. With your free hand or the tip of a crochet hook, pull a loop through the circle.

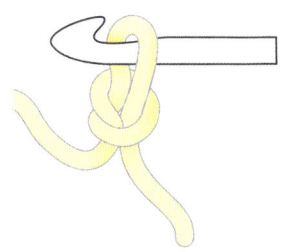

2 Put the hook into the loop and pull gently so that it forms a loose loop on the hook.

Yarn round hook (yrh)

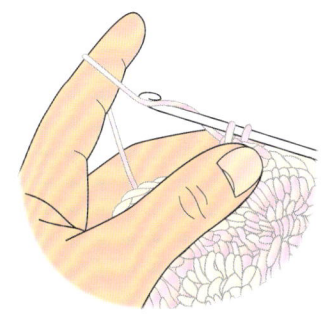

To create a stitch, catch the yarn from behind with the hook pointing upward. As you gently pull the yarn through the loop on the hook, turn the hook so it faces downward and slide the yarn through the loop. The loop on the hook should be kept loose enough for the hook to slide through easily.

Magic ring

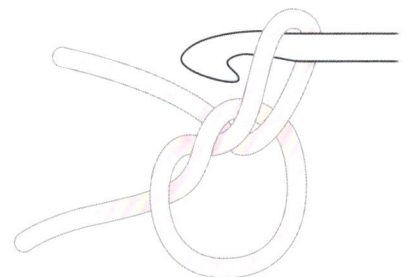

This is a useful starting technique if you do not want a visible hole in the centre of your round. Loop the yarn around your finger, insert the hook through the ring, yarn round hook, pull through the ring to make the first chain. Work the number of stitches required into the ring and then pull the end to tighten the centre ring and close the hole.

Chain (ch)

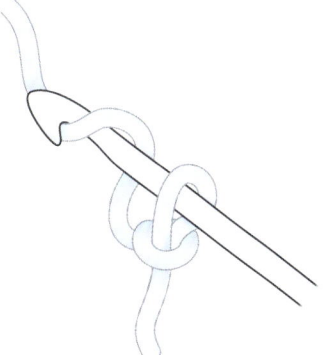

1 Using the hook, wrap the yarn round the hook ready to pull it through the loop on the hook.

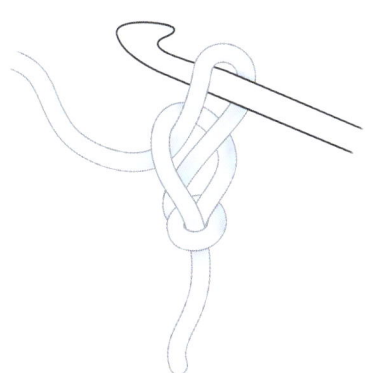

2 Pull through, creating a new loop on the hook. Continue in this way to create a chain of the required length.

Counting chains

To count chains in a foundation chain, lay the chain out on a flat surface with the right side facing you and count each 'V' as one chain. Always count chains from the front of the chain (the end nearest to the hook) and do not count the loop on the hook as one chain.

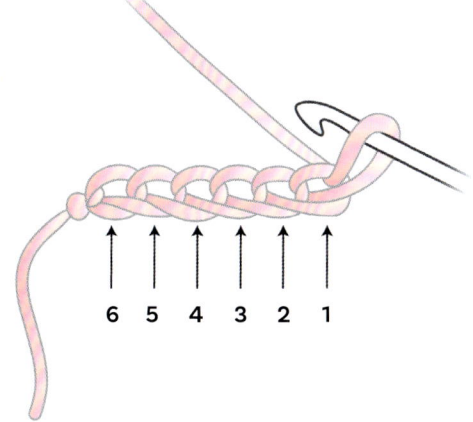

techniques

Chain ring

If you are crocheting a round shape, one way of starting off is by crocheting a number of chains following the instructions in your pattern, and then joining them into a circle.

1 Using the hook, wrap the yarn round the hook ready to pull it through the loop on the hook.

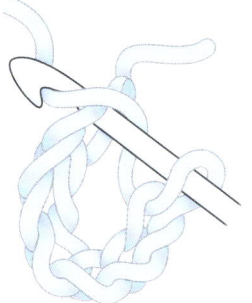

2 Pull the yarn through the chain and through the loop on your hook at the same time, thereby creating a slip stitch and forming a circle. You now have a chain ring ready to work stitches into as instructed in the pattern.

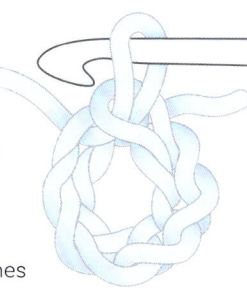

Chain space (ch sp)

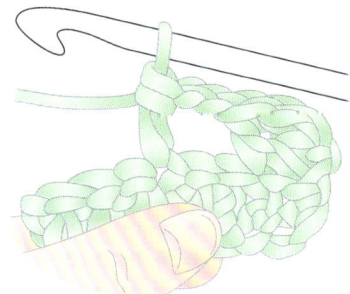

1 A chain space is the space that has been made under a chain in the previous round or row, and falls in between other stitches.

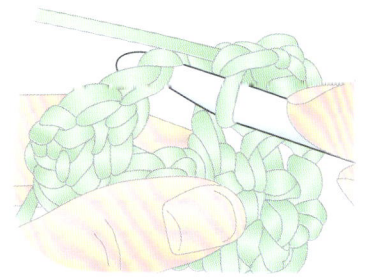

2 Stitches into a chain space are made directly into the hole created under the chain and not into the chain stitches themselves.

Making rows

When making straight rows you turn the work at the end of each row and make a turning chain to create the height you need for the stitch you are working with, as for making rounds.

Double crochet = 1 chain
Half treble crochet = 2 chains
Treble crochet = 3 chains
Double treble = 4 chains

Making rounds

When working in rounds the work is not turned, so you are always working from one side. Depending on the pattern you are working, a 'round' can be square. Start each round by making one or more chains to create the height you need for the stitch you are working:

Double crochet = 1 chain
Half treble crochet = 2 chains
Treble crochet = 3 chains
Double treble = 4 chains

Work the required stitches to complete the round. At the end of the round, slip stitch into the top of the chain to close the round.

Continous spiral

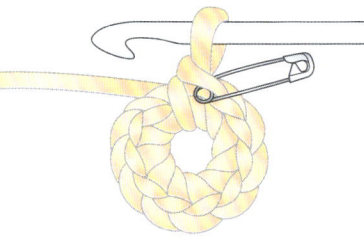

If you work in a spiral you do not need a turning chain. After completing the base ring, place a stitch marker in the first stitch and then continue to crochet around. When you have made a round and reached the point where the stitch marker is, work this stitch, take out the stitch marker from the previous round and put it back into the first stitch of the new round. A safety pin or piece of yarn in a contrasting colour makes a good stitch marker.

Slip stitch (sl st)

A slip stitch doesn't create any height and is often used as the last stitch to create a smooth and even round or row.

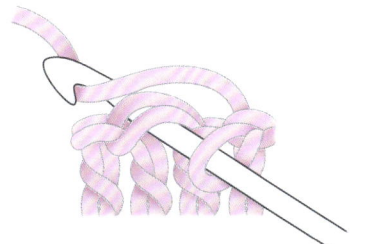

1 To make a slip stitch: first put the hook through the work, yarn round hook.

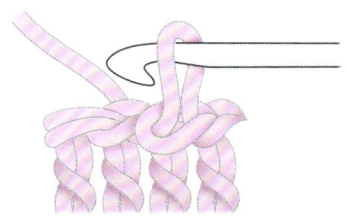

2 Pull the yarn through both the work and through the loop on the hook at the same time, so you will have 1 loop on the hook.

Working into top of stitch

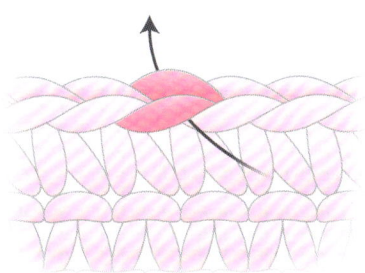

Unless otherwise directed, always insert the hook under both of the two loops on top of the stitch – this is the standard technique.

Working into front loop of stitch (FLO)

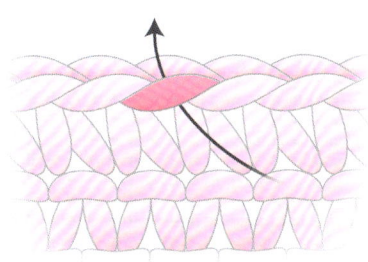

To work into the front loop of a stitch, pick up the front loop from underneath at the front of the work.

Working into back loop of stitch (BLO)

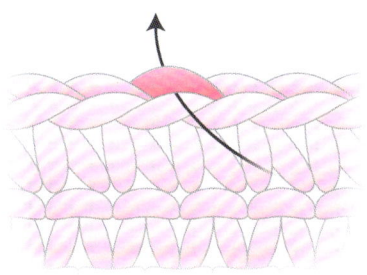

To work into the back loop of the stitch, insert the hook between the front and the back loop, picking up the back loop from the front of the work.

Back post stitch

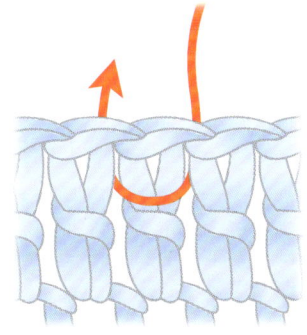

Instead of inserting the hook under or into the 'V' of the required stitch, insert it from the back around the vertical part (the post) of the stitch from the row below.

Tension (gauge)

While specific tension (exactly how loose or tight your crocheted fabric is) isn't essential for these projects, it's important your crocheted fabric is even and doesn't have large gaps. Before you start a project you can make a small swatch, such as 20 stitches by 20 rows in double crochet (US single crochet), to see how the finished crocheted fabric will look with the chosen hook and yarn. If your crocheted fabric is very loose with large gaps, you'll need to use a smaller hook. If the fabric is very tight and difficult to work, use a larger hook. You can experiment by making swatches with different size hooks until you have created a crocheted fabric you're happy with. Use this hook for the project.

Double crochet (dc)

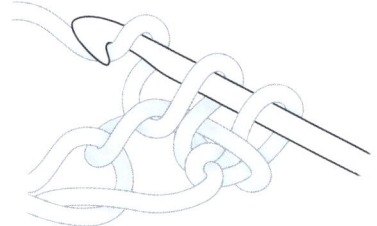

1 Insert the hook into your work, yarn round hook and pull the yarn through the work only. You will then have 2 loops on the hook.

2 Yarn round hook again and pull through the two loops on the hook. You will then have 1 loop on the hook.

Half treble crochet (htr)

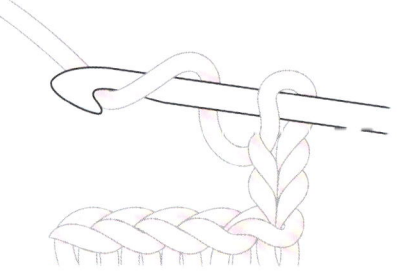
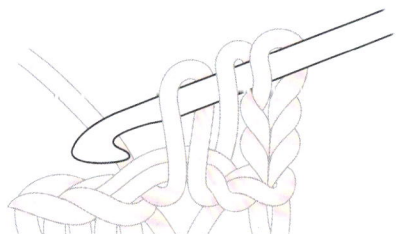
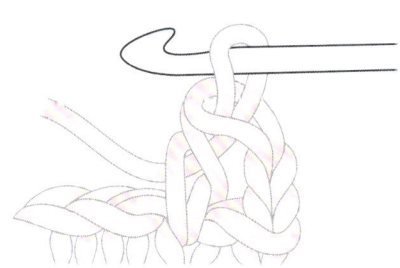

1 Before inserting the hook into the work, wrap the yarn round the hook and put the hook through the work with the yarn wrapped around.

2 Yarn round hook again and pull through the first loop on the hook. You now have 3 loops on the hook.

3 Yarn round hook and pull the yarn through all 3 loops. You will be left with 1 loop on the hook.

Treble crochet (tr)

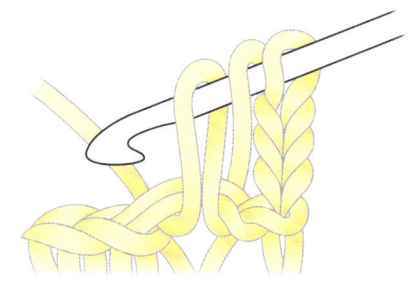
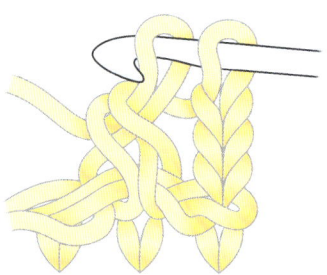

1 Before inserting the hook into the work, wrap the yarn round the hook. Put the hook through the work with the yarn wrapped around, yarn round hook again and pull through the first loop on the hook. You now have 3 loops on the hook.

2 Yarn round hook again, pull the yarn through the first 2 loops on the hook. You now have 2 loops on the hook.

3 Yarn round hook, pull the yarn through 2 loops again. You will be left with 1 loop on the hook.

Double treble (dtr)

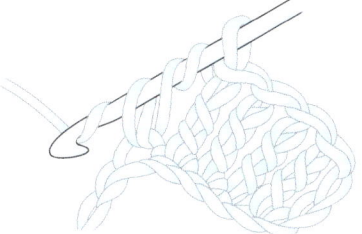

Yarn round hook twice, insert the hook into the stitch, yarn round hook, pull a loop through (4 loops on hook), yarn round hook, pull the yarn through 2 stitches (3 loops on hook), yarn round hook, pull a loop through the next 2 stitches (2 loops on hook), yarn round hook, pull a loop through the last 2 stitches. You will be left with 1 loop on the hook.

Increasing

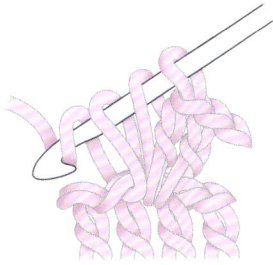

Make two or three stitches into one stitch or space from the previous row. The illustration shows a treble crochet increase being made.

Decreasing

You can decrease by either missing the next stitch and continuing to crochet, or by crocheting two or more stitches together. The basic technique for crocheting stitches together is the same, no matter which stitch you are using. The following example shows dc2tog.

Double crochet two stitches together (dc2tog)

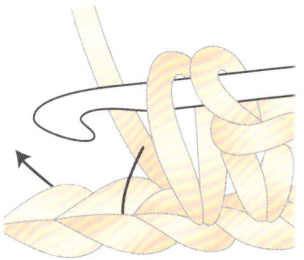
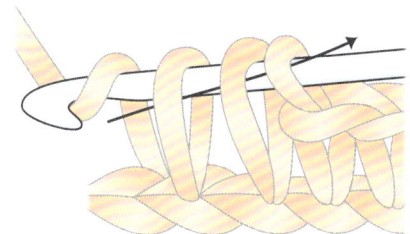

1 Insert the hook into your work, yarn round hook and pull the yarn through the work (2 loops on hook). Insert the hook in next stitch, yarn round hook and pull the yarn through.

2 Yarn round hook again and pull through all 3 loops on the hook. You will then have 1 loop on the hook.

Joining yarn at the end of a row or round

You can use this technique when changing colour, or when joining in a new ball of yarn as one runs out.

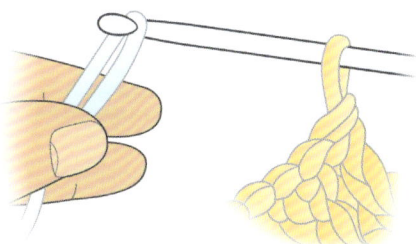
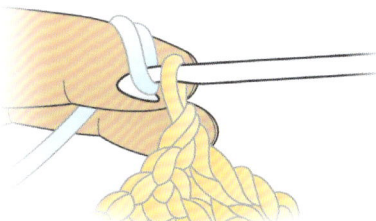

1 Keep the loop of the old yarn on the hook. Drop the tail and catch a loop of the strand of the new yarn with the crochet hook.

2 Draw the new yarn through the loop on the hook, keeping the old loop drawn tight and continue as instructed in the pattern.

Joining in new yarn after fastening off

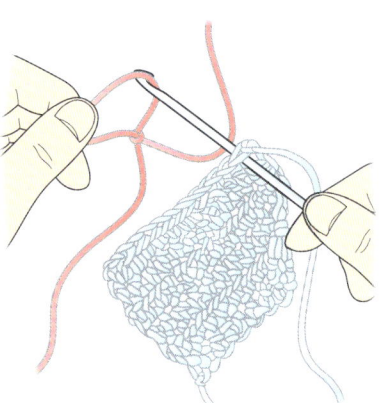
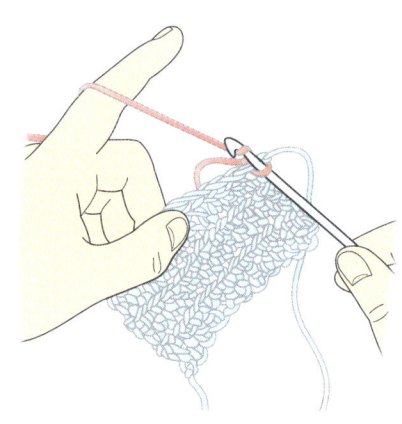

1 Fasten off the old colour (see below). Make a slip knot with the new colour (see page 115). Insert the hook into the stitch at the beginning of the next row, then through the slip knot.

2 Draw the loop of the slip knot through to the front of the work. Carry on working using the new colour, following the instructions in the pattern.

Enclosing a yarn tail

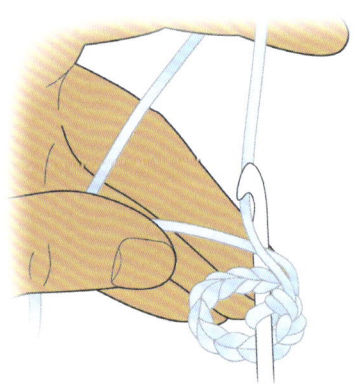

You may find that the yarn tail gets in the way as you work; you can enclose this into the stitches as you go by placing the tail at the back as you wrap the yarn. This also saves having to sew this tail end in later.

Fastening off

When you have finished crocheting, you need to fasten off the stitches to stop all your work unravelling.

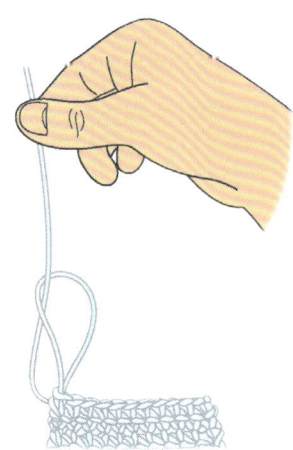

Draw up the final loop of the last stitch to make it bigger. Cut the yarn, leaving a tail of approximately 10cm (4in) - unless a longer end is needed for sewing up. Pull the tail all the way through the loop and pull the loop up tightly.

Sewing in yarn ends

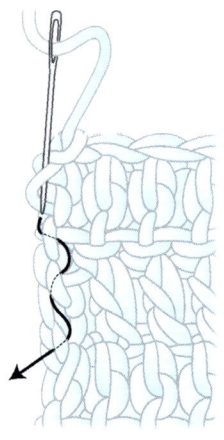

It is important to weave in the tail ends of the yarn so that they are secure and your crochet won't unravel. Thread a yarn needle with the tail end of yarn. On the wrong side, take the needle through the crochet one stitch down on the edge, then take it through the stitches, working in a gentle zig-zag. Work through four or five stitches then return in the opposite direction. Remove the needle, pull the crochet gently to stretch it and trim the end.

Blocking

Crochet can tend to curl, so to make flat pieces stay flat you may need to block them. Pin the piece out to the correct size and shape on an ironing board or some soft foam mats (such as the ones sold as children's play mats). Spray the crochet with water and leave it to dry completely before unpinning and removing from the board or mats.

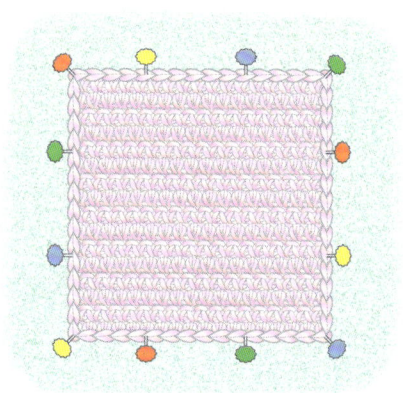

Mattress stitch

Using mattress stitch creates an invisible seam that is perfect for sewing together different crocheted pieces or granny squares. It is worked from the right side.

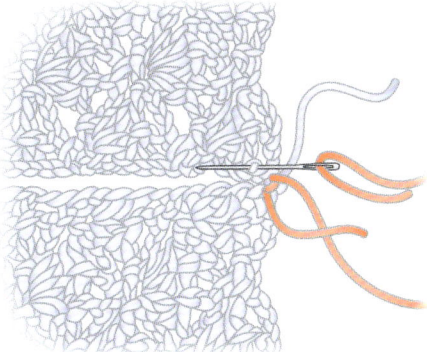

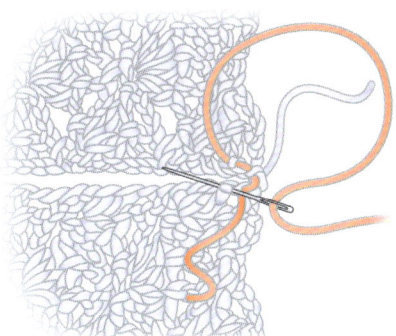

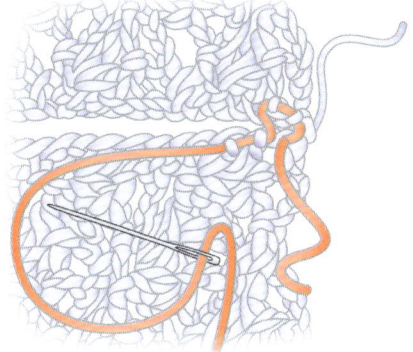

1 Line up the two pieces – pin them together if it helps make them more secure. Thread a tail of yarn in the same colour as the pieces you're joining into a yarn sewing needle. Pick up a loop on the other side with the yarn sewing needle at a horizontal angle (90 degree angle) to the pattern and draw the yarn through loosely.

2 Pick up a loop on the corresponding side of the other piece just inside the edge and draw through the yarn. Leave the loops loose and don't draw them through tightly.

3 Pick up the next loop approx 1cm (½in) along on the same side and draw through the yarn.

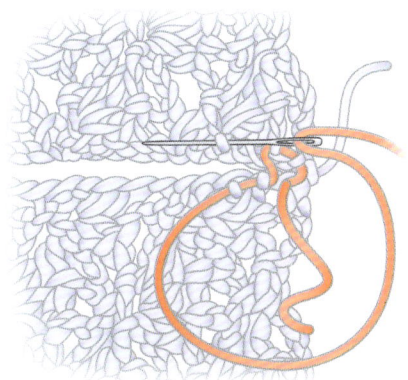

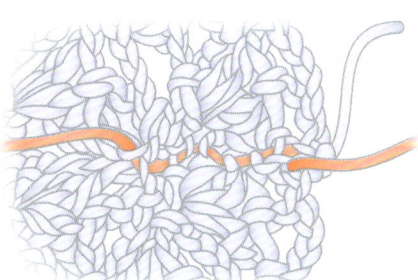

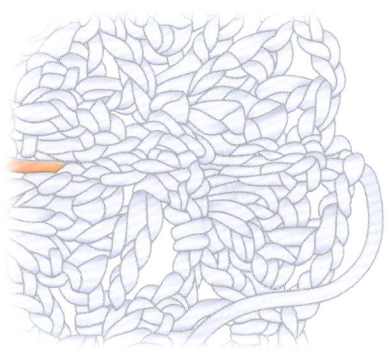

4 Pick up a loop on the corresponding side of the other piece just inside the edge and draw through the yarn. Leave the loops loose and don't draw them through tightly.

5 Repeat steps 3 and 4. When you have about 6 loops, hold the pieces firmly in place and pull the thread to draw the loose loops and bind the edging together.

6 Continue in this way, repeating steps 3, 4 and 5 until the seam is joined. This will create an invisible seam on the right side of the work.

Making a double crochet seam or slip stitch seam
With a double crochet seam you join two pieces together using a crochet hook and working a double crochet stitch through both pieces, instead of sewing them together with a tail of yarn and a yarn sewing needle. This makes a quick and strong seam and gives a slightly raised finish to the edging. For a less raised seam, follow the same basic technique, but work each stitch in slip stitch rather than double crochet.

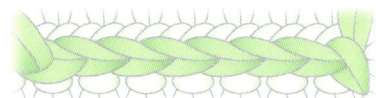
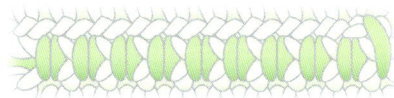

1 Start by lining up the two pieces with wrong sides together. Insert the hook in the top 2 loops of the stitch of the first piece, then into the corresponding stitch on the second piece.

2 Complete the double crochet stitch as normal and continue on the next stitches as directed in the pattern. This gives a raised effect if the double crochet stitches are made on the right side of the work.

3 You can work with the wrong side of the work facing (with the pieces right side facing) if you don't want this effect and it still creates a good strong join.

Join-as-you-go method for granny squares

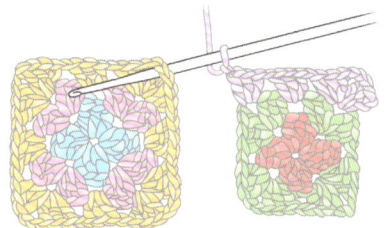
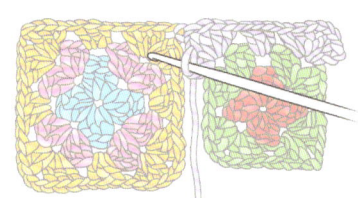
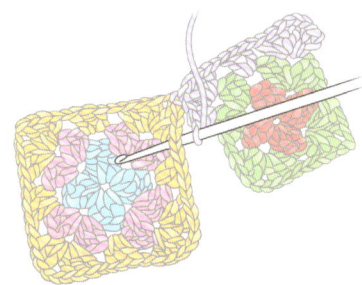

1 Work the first side of the current square including the first corner grouping (first set of 3htr or 3tr), then instead of making ch2 for the corner space, insert the hook into the corner space of the starting square from underneath as shown.

2 1dc into the corner space of the starting square (counts as first of 2-ch for the corner space), ch1, then work the second 3htr or 3tr grouping into the corner space of the current square as usual.

3 To continue joining the squares together, instead of ch1, work 1dc into the next side space of the starting square.

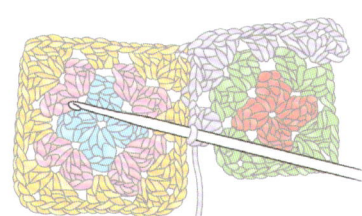
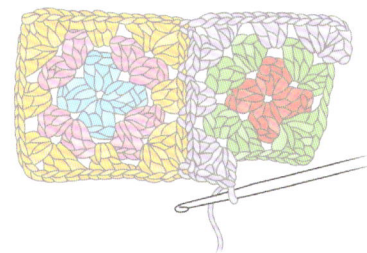
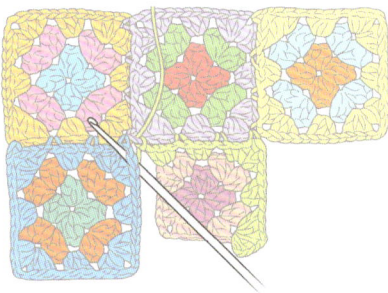

4 Work 3htr or 3tr in the next side space of the current square. Continue replacing each ch-1 at the sides of the current square with 1dc into the next side space of the starting square, and replacing the first of the ch-2 at the corner space of the current square with 1dc into the corner space of the starting square.

5 When the current square is joined to the starting square along one side, continue around and finish the final round of the current square as normal.

6 When joining a current square to two previous squares, replace both corner ch of the current square with 1dc into each adjoining square.

Surface crochet

Surface crochet is a simple way to add extra decoration to a finished item, working slip stitches over the surface of the fabric.

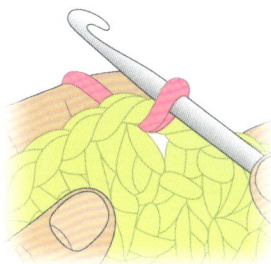 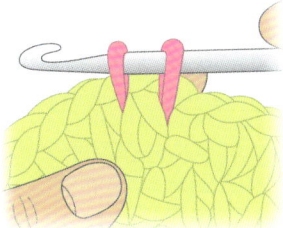 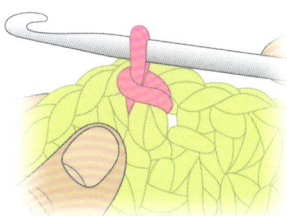

1 Using a contrast yarn, make a slip knot (see page 115). Holding the yarn with the slip knot behind the work and the hook in front, insert the hook between two stitches from front to the back and catch the slip knot behind the work with the hook. Draw the slip knot back through, so there is 1 loop on the hook at the front of the work

2 Insert the hook between the next 2 stitches, yarn round hook and draw a loop through to the front. You will now have 2 loops on the hook.

3 Pull the first loop on the hook through the second loop to complete the first slip stitch on the surface of the work. Repeat steps 2 and 3 to make the next slip stitch. To join two ends with an invisible join, cut the yarn and thread onto a yarn needle. Insert the needle up through the last stitch, into the first stitch as if you were crocheting it, then into the back loop of the previous stitch. Fasten off on the wrong side.

Crab stitch

This is simply double crochet worked backwards to give a twisted edge. Crab stitch spreads the edge slightly, so there's no need to crease to turn a corner. If a straight edge flutes, either miss the occasional stitch or use a smaller hook.

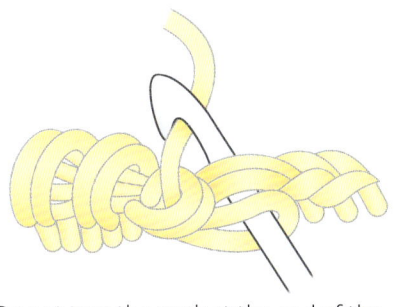

Do not turn the work at the end of the last row. Insert the hook in the last stitch to the right, yarn round hook, and pull through to make two loops twisted on the hook. Yarn round hook again and pull through making one loop on the hook. Repeat in the stitches along the edge or in row ends if necessary.

Popcorn

A popcorn differs from a cluster in that it is made up of complete stitches that are joined at the top. This example shows a popcorn made with four treble stitches worked into a foundation chain, but a popcorn can be worked into any stitch or space and can be made up of any practical number or combination of stitches. It is abbreviated as 'PC'.

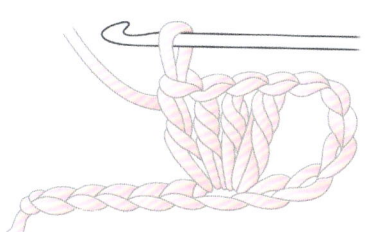 

1 Inserting the hook in the same place each time, work 4 complete trebles.

2 Slip the hook out of the last loop and insert it into the top of the first stitch.

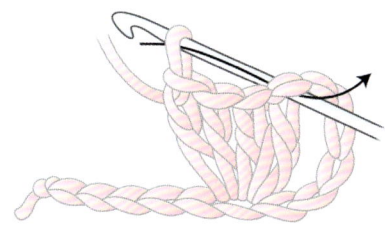 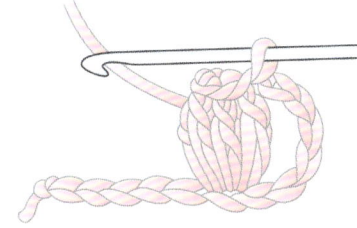

3 Then insert the hook into the loop of the last stitch again. Yarn round hook and pull it through as indicated.

4 This makes one complete popcorn.

techniques 123

Puff stitch

A puff stitch is a padded stitch worked by creating several loops on the hook before completing the stitch. The basic principle is always the same, but you can repeat steps 1 and 2 fewer times to make a smaller puff. Sometimes a chain is worked at the end to secure the puff. It is abbreviated as 'PS'.

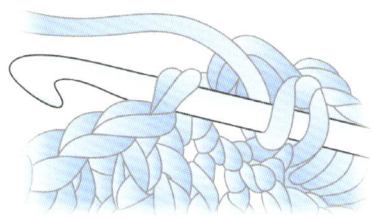

1 Yarn round hook, and insert the hook into the next stitch or space.

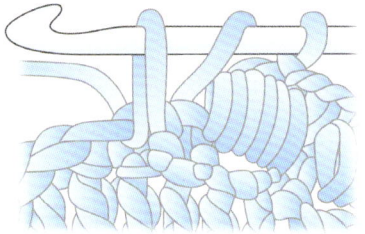

2 Yarn round hook again and draw through, keeping the loops of yarn long.

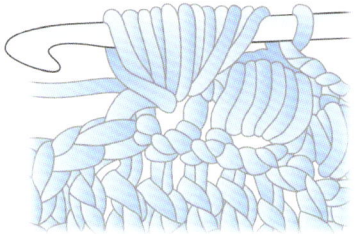

3 Repeat steps 1 and 2 five more times, keeping the loops long each time. There will be 13 loops on the hook.

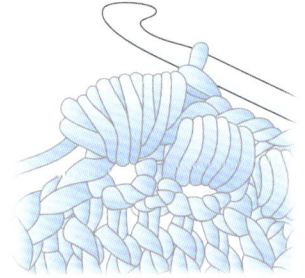

4 Yarn round hook and draw through all the loops on the hook.

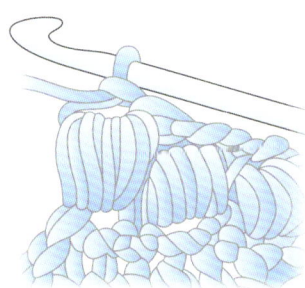

5 Yarn round hook, and draw through the single loop on the hook to make a chain and secure the puff stitch.

Bobble

Bobbles are created when working on wrong-side rows and the bobble is then pushed out towards the right-side row. This is a four-treble cluster bobble (4trCL).

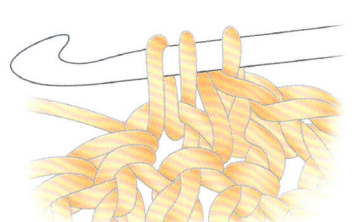

1 Yarn round hook and then insert the hook in the stitch, yarn round hook and pull the yarn through the work.

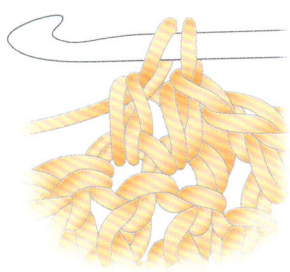

2 Yarn round hook and pull the yarn through the first 2 loops on the hook (2 loops on hook).

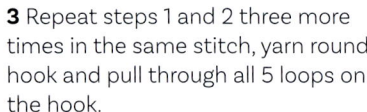

3 Repeat steps 1 and 2 three more times in the same stitch, yarn round hook and pull through all 5 loops on the hook.

4 You can also make 1 chain to complete the bobble.

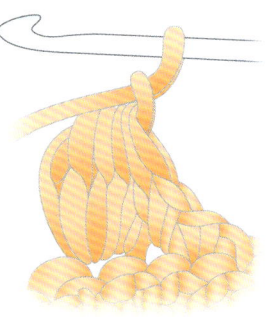

Cluster

Clusters are groups of stitches, with each stitch only partly worked and then all joined at the top to create a particular pattern or shape. They are most effective when made using a longer stitch, such as treble. This is a two-treble cluster, which is abbreviated as '2trCL'.

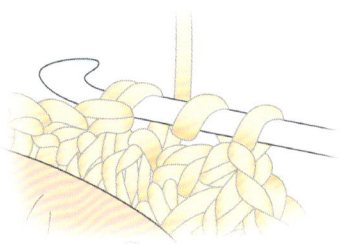

1 Yarn round hook, insert the hook in the stitch (or space).

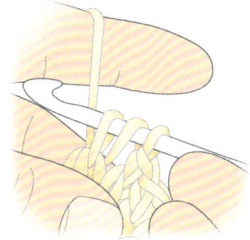

2 Yarn round hook, pull the yarn through the work (3 loops on the hook).

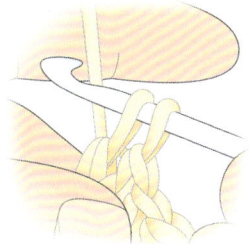

3 Yarn round hook, pull the yarn through 2 loops on the hook (2 loops on the hook).

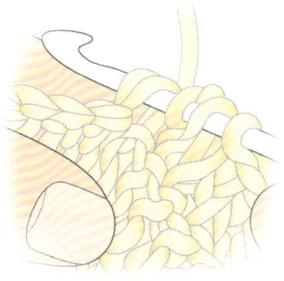

4 Yarn round hook, insert the hook in the same stitch (or space).

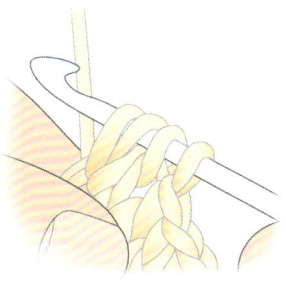

5 Yarn round hook, pull the yarn through the work (4 loops on the hook).

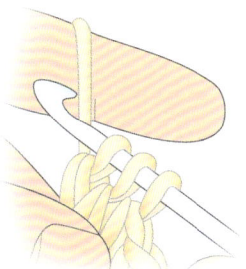

6 Yarn round hook, pull the yarn through 2 loops on the hook (3 loops on the hook).

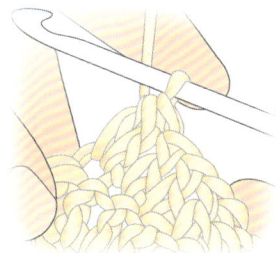

7 Yarn round hook, pull the yarn through all 3 loops on the hook (1 loop on the hook).

Loop stitch

1 With the yarn over the left index finger, insert the hook into the next stitch and draw two strands through the stitch (take the first strand from under the index finger and at the same time take the second strand from over the index finger).

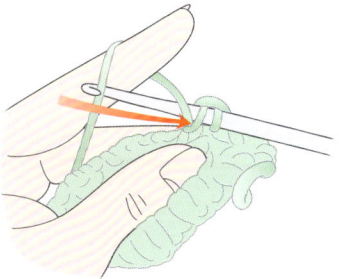

2 Pull the yarn to tighten the loop, forming a 4-cm (1½-in) loop on the index finger. Remove your finger from the loop, put the loop to the back of the work, yarn round hook and pull through 3 loops on the hook (1 loop stitch made on right side of work).

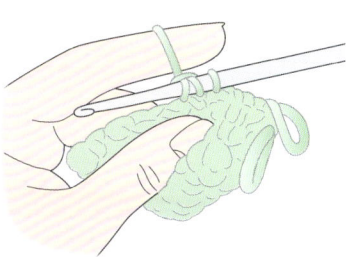

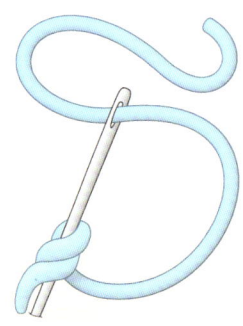

French knots
Bring the yarn needle up to the surface at the position of the knot. Holding the yarn taut, wrap it two or three times around the tip of the needle. Continue holding the yarn under tension as you pass the needle back down through the fabric close to the entry point. The yarn will pull through the wraps and they will form a knot that sits on the surface of the crocheted fabric.

Crochet stitch conversion chart
Crochet stitches are worked in the same way in both the UK and the USA, but the stitch names are not the same and identical names are used for different stitches. Below is a list of the UK terms used in this book, and the equivalent US terms.

UK TERM	US TERM
double crochet (dc)	single crochet (sc)
half treble (htr)	half double crochet (hdc)
treble (tr)	double crochet (dc)
double treble (dtr)	treble (tr)
tension	gauge
yarn round hook (yrh)	yarn over hook (yoh)

Abbreviations

BLO	back loop only
BP	back post
ch	chain
ch sp	chain space
CLr	cluster
cont	continu(e)ing
dc	double crochet
dc2tog	work 2 double crochet stitches together (decrease 1 st)
dtr	double treble
FLO	front loop only
htr	half treble
inc	increase
opp	opposite
PC	popcorn
prev	previous
PS	puff stitch
rep	repeat
RS	right side
slst	slip stitch
st(s)	stitch(es)
tog	together
tr	treble
WS	wrong side
yrh	yarn round hook

Suppliers

We cannot cover all stockists here, so please explore the local yarn shops and online retailers in your own country. If you wish to substitute a different yarn for the one recommended in the pattern, try the Yarnsub website for suggestions: www.yarnsub.com.

UK

LoveCrafts
Online sales
www.lovecrafts.com

Wool
Yarn, hooks
Store in Bath
+44 (0)1225 469144
www.woolbath.co.uk

Wool Warehouse
Online sales
www.woolwarehouse.co.uk

Laughing Hens
Online sales
Tel: +44 (0) 1829 740903
www.laughinghens.com

John Lewis
Yarns and craft supplies
Telephone numbers of stores on website
www.johnlewis.com

Hobbycraft
Yarns, twig wreath bases
www.hobbycraft.co.uk

USA

LoveCrafts
Online sales
www.lovecrafts.com

Knitting Fever Inc.
www.knittingfever.com

WEBS
www.yarn.com

Jo-Ann Fabric and Craft Stores
Yarns and craft supplies
www.joann.com

Michaels
Craft supplies
www.michaels.com

Australia

Black Sheep Wool 'n' Wares
Retail store and online
Tel: +61 (0)2 6779 1196
www.blacksheepwool.com.au

Sun Spun
Retail store (Canterbury, Victoria) and online
Tel: +61 (0)3 9830 1609
www.sunspun.com.au

Acknowledgements

Firstly, I am so very grateful for the continued support and patience from everyone involved at CICO Books. Thank you for believing in me and wanting to share my love of crochet and bright quirky designs in book form. You have made a dream of mine come true!

A huge thank you to Hobbycraft and Rico Design for all the beautiful yarn and material support needed to create my designs. It has been a pleasure as always using your gorgeous products.

I am endlessly grateful for the support of my four daughters who fill my life with pure happiness. They always want to be involved with every new project. I am so proud of them, and so very happy that they are interested in something that means so much to me.

I'd like to thank my partner, Chris, who is always more than happy to listen to my weird and crazy ideas and has supported me every step of my journey this past year. You never tire of showing interest in what I do and I am so thankful of the little pushes that you give me to achieve more of what I love.

Last but certainly not least; I am so thankful of all my yarn loving followers on my social media pages, who have supported me from day one. I am honoured by every like, message and share, every pattern and book sale. I would not be where I am now without your support.

Index

abbreviations 126
acrylic yarn 9

back post stitch 117
Bee and Flower Mobile 86-89
Blanket, Under the Rainbow 40-43
blocking 120
Blooming Lovely Flower Pot 94-97
bobbles 124
Bookmarks 50-52
bottle covers
   Little House Hot Water Bottle Cover 66-68
   Strawberry Water Bottle Cover 78-80

Caterpillar Draught Excluder 32-33
chain (ch) 115
   counting chains 115
chain ring 116
chain space (ch sp) 116
clusters 125
cotton yarn 9
crab stitch 123
Cushion, Flower 14-16

Daisy Chain Bunting 102-103
Daisy Chain Mirror 98-99
decreasing 119
double crochet (dc) 118
double crochet two stitches together (dc2tog) 119
double treble (dtr) 119

equipment 8-9

fastening off 120
Flower Cushion 14-16
Flower Square Wall Tidy 37-39
Fridge Magnets 60-62
Frilly Crochet Chain 104-105

garlands and bunting
   Daisy Chain Bunting 102-103
   Frilly Crochet Chain 104-105
   Roses Garland 100-101
Gnome Sweet Gnome Bookends 72-75
Gnome's Washing Wreath 110-113
granny squares, join-as-you-go method 122
Granny Square Sofa Tidy 34-36
Granny Stitch Place Mats and Coasters 30-31

half treble crochet (htr) 118
holding
   hook 114
   yarn 114

hooks 8
   ergonomic 8
   holding 114
   size 8, 9

increasing 119

Jam Jar Covers 17-19

Ladybird and Flower Coasters 63-65
Lavender Heart 56-57
left-handed crocheters 114
Little House Hot Water Bottle Cover 66-68
loop stitch 125

magic ring 115
mattress stitch 121
Mug Cosy 58-59
Mushroom & Acorn Storage Baskets 24-26
Mushroom Home Keyring 76-77
Mushroom Wall Décor 90-93

Peg Dolls 53-55
Pencil Toppers 69-71
pins 9
popcorns 123
puff stitch 124

Rainbow Rug 27-29
Rainbow Wreath 106-109
Roses Garland 100-101
rounds, making 116
rows, making 116

scissors 8
seams
   double crochet seam 122
   slip stitch seam 122
slip knot 115
slip stitch (sl st) 117
Snail Doorstop 22-23
spiral, continuous 116
stitch conversion chart 126
stitch markers 9
storage
   Flower Square Wall Tidy 37-39
   Granny Square Sofa Tidy 34-36
   Mushroom & Acorn Storage Baskets 24-26
   Tulips Stationery Pot 30-32
Strawberry Water Bottle Cover 78-80
Sunshine and Snails Game 81-83
suppliers 127
surface crochet 123

table settings
   Granny Stitch Place Mats and Coasters 30-31
   Ladybird and Flower Coasters 63-65
   Table Runner 44-45
tape measure 9
Tea Towel Tidy 12-13
techniques 114-125
tension (gauge) 117
tension swatch 117
Tissue Box Cover 46-47
treble crochet (tr) 118
Tulips Stationery Pot 20-21

Under the Rainbow Blanket 40-43

working into back loop of stitch (BLO) 117
working into front loop of stitch (FLO) 117
working into top of stitch 117
wreaths
   Gnome's Washing Wreath 110-113
   Rainbow Wreath 106-109

yarn 9
   enclosing yarn tail 120
   fastening off 120
   fibres 9
   holding 114
   joining new yarn 119, 120
   suppliers 127
   weaving in yarn ends 120
   weights 9
yarn round hook (yrh) 115
yarn needle 9